Renita Boyle gained a BA (Hons) in Theology, focusing her thesis on child sexual exploitation. She is a former and founding editor of Viva Network's *Children at Risk* magazine. Renita is co-author of BRF's *Understanding Compassion*, which was published in partnership with *Compassion UK* in 2004. She is an experienced children's worker and storyteller and is currently, among other projects, producing issues-based curriculum for CURBS (Children in Urban Situations). Renita is married to Eric and they have one young son, Jude.

D1393035

Published by
The Bible Reading Fellowship
First Floor, Elsfield Hall
15–17 Elsfield Way, Oxford OX2 8FG
Website: www.brf.org.uk

ISBN 978 1 84101 491 3
First published 2007
10 9 8 7 6 5 4 3 2 1 0

Acknowledgments
Scripture quotations are taken from the Contemporary English Version of the Bible published
by HarperCollins Publishers, copyright © 1991, 1992, 1995 American Bible Society.

A catalogue record for this book is available from the British Library

Printed in Singapore by Craft Print International Ltd

Parable Fun
for Little Ones

10 sessions of pick-and-mix stories and activities for under-fives

Renita Boyle

For Jude, whose name means 'praise'

Contents

Prayer pocket templates

Home and away sheets

Rhyme time poems

Index

Foreword

I have taught Sunday school for more years than I care to remember and, when in Christian bookshops, I scour the shelves for ideas of how to present the old, old story in new and interesting ways. The gospel doesn't change, but children do—and it's the teacher's job to run to keep up with them. I'm grateful that Renita Boyle has done some running for me, and that I'll be able to use the fruits of her efforts with the children I teach, who are aged five and under.

In *Parable Fun for Little Ones* the author takes ten of Jesus' parables and creates a whole ménage of teaching activities around them. For example, each story begins with a thoughtful welcome activity, just enough to whet the children's appetites for what is to come, yet not so demanding that a shy child will crawl into his or her shell and remain there for the rest of the session. The Story Sack will have them on the edge of their seats as they wait to see what delights it contains, and Rhyme Time will encourage boys and girls to chant the story long after they go home. Renita Boyle's recognition that rhyme is a really valuable teaching tool when working with under-fives adds value to the lessons. It's a pity not to make use of what really works, and rhythm, rhyme and children just go together. After all, we still remember nursery rhymes learnt when we were three and four years old!

While the lessons follow a pattern and children will know roughly what is coming next, the activities themselves are so amazingly varied that there is no possibility of boredom—none whatsoever. In addition, although the activities in *Parable Fun for Little Ones* really are fun, they all earn their keep in terms of Bible teaching. Not one is a time filler or merely for entertainment.

While each parable, complete with all its activities, is intended to be used as a unit, the material could equally well be split over several sessions to good effect, and the fact that each activity is timed is a real bonus.

Parable Fun for Little Ones is not for the faint-hearted as each lesson requires quite a bit of preparation, but teaching the gospel to young children is not for the faint-hearted either. Those who take on this responsibility know its importance and are prepared to put some effort into it. Renita Boyle has done a great deal of work and those who add their effort to hers will, I'm sure, reap blessings.

Irene Howat, author and storyteller

Introduction

Who is Silly Billy? What are Mick and Mac building? Where is Little Lamb? Why is Grandma Guddle in such a muddle? How will Farmer Friendly get her crops to grow? What did Jolly Molly find? Will Good Sammy come to the rescue? What is Tom Farmer waiting for? Will Tired Tim ever get any sleep?

The answers to these questions and many more are contained in *Parable Fun for Little Ones*, a flexible, fun-filled exploration of Jesus' parables for use with preschoolers. Whether you are a parent, grandparent, Sunday school teacher, minister, nursery school teacher or carer, you are sure to find *Parable Fun for Little Ones* a great tool for spiritual and moral development.

The book contains stories and methods for telling them, songs and finger rhymes, crafts and games, role play, snack ideas, prayer activities, Bible verses with actions and family fun activities to do at home.

Its pick-and-mix approach makes it ideal for use in church and out: in crèche, playgroups, nursery schools, Sunday schools, family services, school assemblies and children's talks, coffee mornings and charity events, or at home.

Parable Fun for Little Ones is both relational and playful. It encourages the fundamental relationships that children have with their primary carers at home, other carers away from home and their peers, and it does so through varied methods of themed play.

The material is in keeping with national guidelines. It will provide opportunities for spiritual and moral development as well as facilitating the fulfilment of early learning goals for ages 3–5, such as:

✪ Communication, language and literacy
✪ Mathematical development
✪ Personal, social, emotional development
✪ Knowledge and understanding of the world
✪ Physical development and movement
✪ Creative, expressive and aesthetic development
✪ Spiritual and moral development

Finally, the book contains an index of themes and activities to help you freely dip in and out of this material and adapt, add or subtract to suit your needs, your children, your timeframe and the physical space.

How to use this book

Health and safety issues are of primary concern when working with children. Before you use this material, please ensure that:

- Child care workers understand child protection procedures and are cleared for work with children.
- There is good communication between parents, carers and child care workers.
- Data protection procedure is followed.
- Children are dressed appropriately for activities and given clear guidance.
- Objects used are age-appropriate and child-safe.
- Food ingredients are appropriate for those with allergies, and food hygiene regulations are followed.

The material in a single session will provide about one and a half hours of activities, although this timescale can be shortened or lengthened by choosing fewer activities or taking longer with an individual activity. A time guide is given with each activity to help in the planning of your session.

Each session is focused on one of Jesus' parables, which is retold in rhyme and explored through any combination of the activities explained below. 'Chat about' questions appear at intervals throughout each session.

Ready, steady, go

Ready, steady, go gives you the following preparation material:

- The 'aim', 'truth' and 'themes' of each session.
- The biblical basis from which the rhyme time parable is derived (based on the Contemporary English Version of the Bible).

Ensure that all helpers understand the aim, truth and themes of the session as well as the structure chosen. Where appropriate, discuss personal learning goals for each child—for example, to help Sally feel more confident or Joe to listen better. If used in a church or club setting, pray for one another, the children and their families.

In a circle

Circle times are particularly effective in developing community, self-esteem, confidence, social skills and cooperation. During the circle time, ensure that:

- The floor space is big enough, and free from obstacles and too many distractions.
- A cushion or chair is provided for each person.
- The storyteller is on a level with the children and can be seen and heard by everyone.
- Helpers are evenly distributed to help where needed.
- Children are given clear guidance on how to minimize safety risks, so that toes and fingers are not stood on.
- The story sack is nearby and only those objects currently in use remain in the circle.
- Young or reluctant children, and those with special needs and their helpers, are welcomed in ways appropriate to the child.
- Everyone is included, everyone belongs and everyone is valued.

Pat-a-pet

Choose an appropriate stuffed animal, beanie doll or puppet to be the pat-a-pet for each session. Ideas for use are included for each session. The pat-a-pet can:

- Give hugs and help with welcomes and waves.
- Demonstrate a request made of the children, such as 'go around the circle to the left' or 'jump over the rope'.
- Be the official turn-taker during circle time. For example, only the person holding the pet may speak, and everyone else must listen. The pat-a-pet may be passed on to someone wishing to speak or as an encouragement to a child who might be reluctant to speak.
- Give encouragement or prizes to those who behave well, achieve a task, improve on a skill or show kindness or helpfulness.

Welcomes and waves

Remembering a child's name is a positive affirmation of self-worth. Ideas for name games, welcomes and waves and name tags are included for each session.

Story sack

The story sack is a large pillowcase or bag containing the props for telling the rhyme time parable. Script and prop ideas are given for each session.

Rhyme time

Each session is focused on one of Jesus' parables. The rhyme time parable is based on a well-known nursery rhyme and told with the help of the story sack. Although the rhyme time parable is not taken directly from the Bible, it is important to help children make the connection to the Bible. This is usefully done by making accessible a child-friendly Bible and encouraging the children to understand the Bible as God's storybook. Relate the rhyme time parable to the Bible by saying, 'This is a story something like one Jesus told. We can find the stories Jesus told in the Bible, God's storybook.'

Up and about with tickle trunk

Up and about activities will allow imaginative and energetic exploration of each parable and attendant themes.

The tickle trunk is a large trunk, plastic container or cardboard box filled with clean and safe dressing-up clothes and props based on the session's parable and theme. The tickle trunk may be used in free play or to help children dramatize the parable in their own way. Children may even participate in decorating the tickle trunk. Specific ideas for the contents of the tickle trunk are given for each session. In general, be on the look out for:

✪ Oversized clothes, such as old suits, bright flowery shirts, bridesmaids' dresses, nightgowns and pyjamas (buttons and zippers may be replaced with Velcro ® for easier handling).
✪ Clothing accessories, such as boots, shoes, hats, scarves, gloves, necklaces, bangles, hats, wigs, slippers and handbags.
✪ Costumes, such as fairies, superheroes and animals.
✪ Uniforms, such as doctor, nurse, fire fighter, police officer, astronaut, racing car driver.

✪ Towels, textured and themed fabrics, headbands with antennae, and umbrellas.
✪ Props such as toy gardening tools, building tools and seaside equipment.

'We can' can

Choose a container with a wide enough mouth for a child's hand to get in, such as a crisps tube. The 'We can' can contains slips of paper with on-the-spot activities that require no special materials, preparation or clean-up. Each activity is related to the parable. A child will choose the activity from the 'We can' can and the helper will read it out and lead it—for example, 'We can sing Old MacDonald', or 'We can grow like a tree'. The 'We can' can is particularly useful during down-times, in-between times or as a distraction from chaos. Ideas for the 'We can' can are included for each session.

Food fun

Food fun gives you a snack idea or recipe related to the session's parable. Children may be involved in preparation or simply enjoy the snack.

Prayer pocket

The prayer pocket is a large manila envelope decorated according to the theme, which contains ideas to help children express themselves in prayer. A variety of prayers and methods for prayer are explored.

Busy box

The busy box is a large box containing craft materials. Ideas for the contents of the busy box and directions for a craft related to the parable are included for each session. It will be useful to:

✪ Protect table and floor surfaces with messy mats, drip sheets or newspaper.
✪ Provide a clearly identified place for projects to dry.
✪ Ensure that there are enough helpers to supervise and that all helpers understand the project instructions.
✪ Help children write their names on projects for easy identification.
✪ Find a way to show the children's work in an eye-catching, eye-level display.

Go game

The go game is an energetic group game or activity related to the session's parable.

Music makers

Music makers provides an idea for a musical activity based on the theme of the parable or ways to incorporate music in the session's other activities.

Memory time

Memory time provides an opportunity to learn a Bible memory verse with simple actions. For each session, you will need to write out the memory verse on a card to display to the children.

Home and Away sheets

A Home and Away sheet is provided for each session. This will enable a good flow of information, foster supportive relationships with primary carers and encourage greater participation. The sheet contains:

✪ Think together (including the biblical basis of the day's parable).
✪ Link together (including an activity linked to the session).
✪ Play together (including a fun activity for all the family).
✪ Pray together (including a simple one-line prayer to say together).

A further sheet with the rhyme time poem is also available for the children to take home if desired.

Jolly Molly May

Ready, steady, go

- ✪ **Aim:** To affirm the joy of knowing Jesus
- ✪ **Truth:** Being friends with Jesus is the best treasure ever
- ✪ **Themes:** Treasure, sea life, happiness and family

Biblical basis: A hidden treasure

Jesus said: The kingdom of heaven is like what happens when someone finds treasure hidden in a field and buries it again. A person like that is happy and goes and sells everything in order to buy that field.

MATTHEW 13:44

In a circle

Name tag crabs

 Time guide: 5 minutes

You will need: A crab name tag for each child (see page 64 for photocopiable template), coloured pens, pencils or crayons, a hole punch, sticky tape, scissors and a length of ribbon

Help the children to cut out and colour their tags and write their names on the front. Place sticky tape toward the top, where you will punch a hole. Loop ribbon through the hole and tie the ends.

Pat-a-pet

Click-clack Crab

 Time guide: 5 minutes

You will need: A crab soft toy or puppet, sand bucket, blue confetti or shredded paper

Hide Click-clack Crab in a sand bucket full of blue confetti or shredded paper. Repeat the following rhyme to introduce Click-clack Crab as a visitor for the day. Talk about crabs and their habitat.

Here is a bucket
Deep and wide.
I wonder what is hidden inside (peep inside).
It's Click-clack Crab without a doubt
Hey, click clack, clack click, come out!

Remove Click-clack Crab from the bucket and scatter the confetti on the children.

Welcomes and waves

X marks the spot

 Time guide: 5 minutes

You will need: Click-clack Crab and a helper to lead

Ask the children to stand up and turn to the right. When you say someone's name, everyone is to repeat the name and take one step around the circle for every beat in it. For example, 'Sam-u-el' would be three steps, 'Sa-rah' two steps, 'Matt' one step, and so on. When you shout 'X marks the spot!' everyone is to sit down where they are as quickly as they can. Continue play until everyone's name has been called. Make sure to include Click-clack Crab in the fun.

Chat about

Chat about what the children like about their names. Does anyone's name have a special meaning or story? Does God know each of us by name?

Story sack

Jolly Molly May

 Time guide: 5 minutes

You will need: Some yellow silk scarves in different shades (sand) and some blue silk scarves (sea), three rag dolls or beanie dolls dressed in summer clothes (Maggie, Milly and Molly May), a seashell, a toy crab and a treasure chest bundled unseen in a yellow silk scarf

You will wear: Sunhat and beach wear

Dress up as if you are going to the beach. Hold the story sack in your lap until everyone in the circle is seated and settled. Instruct the children that they are not to move from where they are sitting unless told to do so. Quietly set up the scene.

Remove the blue silk scarves one at a time and ruffle them out on the floor like ocean waves. Remove the yellow silk scarves one at a time and create a beach and sand dunes. Hide the treasure chest unseen in a yellow silk scarf and place it among the dunes. Tell the following story, following the directions in roman (upright) type.

Rhyme time

Jolly Molly May

 Time guide: 10 minutes

Maggie and Milly and jolly Molly May
(Remove Maggie, Milly and Molly May one at a time and place them on the beach)
Went to the beach to play one day.

Maggie found a shell that sang like the sea
(Remove the shell and place it next to Maggie's ear),
Went to show her mum, happy as could be.
(Put Maggie and her shell out of sight behind your back)

Milly found a crab scuttling all around
(Remove the crab from the story sack and place it next to Milly),
Went to tell her dad what she had found.
(Milly runs out of sight behind your back in one direction and the crab in the other)

I wonder, do you wonder, jolly Molly May,
(Pick up Jolly Molly May as if speaking to her)
What did you find on the beach that day?

Molly found a chest hidden in the sand
(Molly May finds the hidden treasure and gets excited),
Discovered it, uncovered it, then buried it again.
(Molly May buries the chest again without opening it)

Molly's got a secret smile upon her face,
Molly's got a treasure and knows its hiding place.
(Molly runs out of sight behind your back)

I wonder, do you wonder what our treasure is?
Jesus is our treasure and we are his!

Chat about

Chat about what the children liked best about this story. Use some of the following wondering questions:

- ✪ I wonder what you would like to find on the beach?
- ✪ I wonder how Molly felt when she found the treasure?
- ✪ I wonder what Molly's treasure was?
- ✪ I wonder why Molly kept the treasure a secret?
- ✪ I wonder what we treasure most?
- ✪ I wonder what Jesus treasures most?
- ✪ I wonder how knowing Jesus is the best treasure ever?

When you are finished, quietly remove the scene, talking about each item as you return it to the story sack.

Up and about with tickle trunk

 Time guide: 10 minutes

You will need: Floppy hats, sunglasses, flip-flops, beach towels, beach toys, seashells and animals, treasure chest, buckets and spades, sandbox

Either encourage the children to play freely with the parable in their own way or choose a cast of children to act out the rhyme time parable.

'We can' can

We can sing 'What shall we do...?'

(Tune: What shall we do with a drunken sailor?)

 Time guide: 5 minutes

You will need: A slip of paper that says: 'We can sing "What shall we do when we go to the seaside?"' and the following words.

What shall we do when we go to the seaside (x 3)
Early in the morning?

Make a castle out of sand...
(x 3, pretending to make a sandcastle)
Put on our very best swimsuits...
(x 3, pretending to dress)
Run and jump in the waves...
(x 3, pretending to splash)
Swim up and down in the sea...
(x 3, pretending to swim)
Look for shells on the seashore...
(x 3, pretending to look)
Go for a walk along the beach...
(x 3, pretending to walk)
Have an ice cream in a cone...
(x 3, pretending to lick)
Watch for boats out in the sea...
(x 3, pretending to spy)
Find some treasure in the sand...
(x 3, pretending to dig)

Choose a child to remove the instructions from the 'We can' can. Read the instructions aloud. Do the chant and rhyme together.

Chat about

Chat about a time when the children went to the seaside. What do they like to do most when they go to the seaside?

Food fun

A day at the beach

 Time guide: 10 minutes

You will need: Beach towels, umbrella, container of sand, seashells, tape of beach sounds, cold fruit juice, ice cream and cones

Spread the towels out on the floor. Open an umbrella and lay it on its side nearby, turn on the beach sounds, place seashells in the area, eat up and clean up.

Chat about

Chat about the kind of things we see, feel, smell, hear, taste when we are at the seaside. What lives in the sea?

Prayer pocket

Seaside prayers

 Time guide: 5 minutes

You will need: A prayer pocket decorated like a seaside bucket, a set of seaside prayer shapes for each child, such as a starfish, fish, seahorse, crab, seashell and treasure chest (see photocopiable sheet on page 69)

Put one set of seaside shapes into the prayer pocket before the session. Recite the rhyme below, asking a child to remove a shape from the prayer pocket. Help the children to thank Jesus for one characteristic that we treasure about him (kind, loving, giving, forgiving, always there and so on). Repeat this exercise until all the shapes are gone and several children have had a chance to pray.

Here is a bucket
Deep and wide.
I wonder what is hidden inside? (peep inside)
It's a [name seaside shape], without a doubt.
Hey, [seaside shape], come on out!

Finish with the prayer below.

Thank you, Jesus, for treasuring us. Help us to treasure you. Amen

Home and away link

Send a sheet of seaside shapes home with each child. 'Home and away' provides a further linked activity.

Busy box

Treasure boxes

Time guide: 10 minutes

You will need: Plain cardboard gift boxes, paint, brushes, pencils, glitter glue, shells, jewels and other decorative materials

Help the children to paint and decorate their boxes. Leave the boxes to dry ready for the children to take home.

Chat about

Chat about what the children would put in a treasure box. What would they like to find in a treasure box?

Go game

Beachcomber

Time guide: 5 minutes

You will need: Beanbags (treasure) and a large playing area

Divide the group into two. One half are beachcombers, the other half are waves. Send the beachcombers to one end of the playing space and the waves to the other. Scatter the beanbags (treasure) in a line in the middle. When the leader says 'Go', the beachcombers rush out, pick up a piece of treasure and try to bring it home before the waves tag them. Reverse teams and play again.

Chat about

Chat about what the children would like to find on a beach. How do they feel when they find rubbish on the beach?

Music makers

Crabs in the bucket

Time guide: 5 minutes

You will need: Seaside themed music

When the music is playing, the children scuttle around sideways in a crab position (bending over frontward or backward with hands and feet on the ground). When the music stops, they stand up, clasp their hands in a circle like a bucket in front of them and remain as still as possible. Anyone who moves has to sit down for the remainder of the game. Play until one child is left standing.

Chat about

Ask the children, if they could be any sea creature, what would they be and why?

Memory time

Time guide: 5 minutes

You will need: The Bible verse 'Your heart will always be where your treasure is' (Matthew 6:21)

Teach the children the following actions. Explain that remembering what is said in the Bible can really help us, and that they are going to try to remember something Jesus said, using both words and actions.

> **Your:** Sweep outwards from left to right with your right hand, palm open and facing upward.
>
> **Heart:** Use your right and left index fingers to draw a heart shape over your own heart.
>
> **Will be where:** Hold your right hand out, palm up.
>
> **Your:** Sweep outwards from left to right with your right hand, palm open and facing upward.
>
> **Treasure:** Hold your hands in loose fists, thumbs lying flat on top. Bring fists together side-by-side, touching heels of hands, knuckles and thumbs.
>
> **Is:** Hold your right hand out, palm up.

Practise the actions to the verse yourself in advance of the session.

Chat about

Chat about how often we think about the things we treasure. How can we make Jesus our best treasure ever?

1

Home and away

Give each child a copy of Home and Away Sheet 1 (see page 74), the Jolly Molly May rhyme time poem (see page 84) and a copy of the seaside shapes (see page 69).

Oats, peas, beans and barley grow

Ready, steady, go

- ✪ **Aim:** To encourage spiritual growth
- ✪ **Truth:** Spiritual growth happens quietly over time
- ✪ **Themes:** Farming, growing, patience, work, animals, seasons

Biblical basis: The growing seeds

Jesus said: God's kingdom is like what happens when a farmer scatters seed in a field. The farmer sleeps at night and is up and around during the day. Yet the seeds keep sprouting and growing, and he doesn't understand how. It is the ground that makes the seeds sprout and grow into plants that produce grain. Then when harvest season comes and the grain is ripe, the farmer cuts it with a sickle.

MARK 4:26–29

In a circle

Name tag cows

 Time guide: 5 minutes

You will need: A cow name tag for each child (see page 64 for photocopiable template), coloured pens, pencils or crayons, a hole punch, sticky tape, scissors and a length of ribbon

Help the children to cut out and colour their tags and write their names on the front. Place sticky tape toward the top, where you will punch a hole. Loop ribbon through the hole and tie the ends.

Pat-a-pet

Clover Cow

 Time guide: 5 minutes

You will need: A cow soft toy or puppet

Introduce Clover Cow to the group as a visitor for the day. Talk about cows.

Welcomes and waves

Hey diddle diddle

 Time guide: 5 minutes

You will need: Clover Cow pat-a-pet, the following rhyme, and a helper to lead

Hey diddle diddle,
[Name a child] had a fiddle
And played us a merry tune.
(Child stands and pretends to fiddle)
(Throw Clover Cow to another child)
[Name the second child] took the chance
to have a small dance
(Child stands and dances)
And Clover jumped over the moon.

Throw Clover Cow to someone else in the circle, repeat the rhyme and do the actions until everyone has had their name called.

Story sack

Oats, peas, beans and barley grow

 Time guide: 5 minutes

You will need: A farmer beanie doll, a blanket, toy cockerel, cow, horse, pig, goat, lamb, hammer and tractor, a Bible

You will wear: A farmer's outfit (dungarees, shirt, boots, hat and so on)

Dress up like a farmer. Hold the story sack in your lap until everyone in the circle is seated and settled. Instruct the children that they are not to move from where they are sitting unless told to do so. Quietly begin.

Rhyme time

Oats, peas, beans and barley grow

 Time guide: 10 minutes

Tell the rhyme time parable, following the directions in roman (upright) type. The rhyme may also be sung to the tune of 'Oats, peas, beans and barley grow'.

Oats, peas, beans and barley grow,
Oats, peas, beans and barley grow.
I wonder, do you wonder how
Oats, peas, beans and barley grow?
(Remove the farmer from the story sack)

First Tom Farmer plants the seed,
(Farmer pretends to scatter seeds)
Then he rests and takes his ease,
(Lay the farmer down, remove the blanket and cover him)
And while he's sleeping peacefully
(Whisper with finger to mouth in a 'hush')
Oats, peas, beans and barley grow.

Cockerel crows to sing the dawn,
(Remove cockerel and set him down)
Wake up, Tom, it's early morn!
(Remove the farmer from under the blanket and stand him up by the cockerel)
Cows need milking in the barn
(Remove cow and put her beside the farmer)
While oats, peas, beans and barley grow.

The horse needs hay, the pigs need corn.
(Remove the horse, then the pig, and place them beside the farmer)
The goat needs grass, the lambs are born.
(Remove the goat, then the lamb, and place them beside the farmer)
The fence needs fixing, the hay is mown
(Remove the hammer, then the tractor, and place them beside the farmer)
While oats, peas, beans and barley grow.

Harvest time is nearly here,
Farmer Tom is full of cheer.
Hey, Tom, is it time to bring
The oats, peas, beans and barley in?

You and I can root and grow,
(Point to the children and then to yourself)
You and I can root and grow.
(Point to the children and then to yourself)
I wonder, do you wonder how
(Shrug shoulders quizzically)
You and I can root and grow?

You and I grow day by day
Listening to what Jesus has to say.
(Pretend to pray)

God's Spirit helps us root and grow
(Remove the Bible and open it)
When Jesus shows us the way to go.

Chat about

Chat about if the children have ever seen crops growing in a field. Use some of the following wondering questions:

- ✪ I wonder if seeds make a noise when they grow?
- ✪ I wonder how we know a seed is growing when it can't yet be seen?
- ✪ I wonder how God helps us to grow in different ways?
- ✪ I wonder how long it takes to grow?

When you are finished, quietly remove the scene, talking about each item as you return it to the story sack.

Up and about with tickle trunk

 Time guide: 10 minutes

You will need: Farm toys: tractors, trailers, machinery, jeeps, barn, house, fences and so on; farm animals: cows, goats, pigs, hens, horses, dog, cat, sheep and so on; farm people: a farmer and his family and so on; farmer's dressing-up clothes: dungarees, wellies, hat and a shirt

Either encourage the children to play freely with the parable in their own way or choose a cast of children to act out the rhyme time parable.

'We can' can

We can make a rain storm

 Time guide: 5 minutes

You will need: The 'We can' can containing directions for 'We can make a rain storm'

Choose a child to remove the instructions from the 'We can' can. Say, 'We can make a rain storm' and ask the children to copy what you do. NB: Count to ten in your head for each action.

1 Rub the palms of your hands together.
2 Pat alternate knees with hands slowly.

3 Pat alternate knees with hands at medium speed.
4 Pat alternate knees with hands quickly.
5 Stamp alternate feet quickly.

Do everything in reverse to make the rain storm stop.

Chat about

Chat about how seeds need rain and sunshine to grow. What happens if there is not enough rain or sunshine to help the plants grow?

Food fun

Farmer Tom's breakfast time

 Time guide: 10 minutes

You will need: Some different kinds of bread, butter, jam, breakfast cereals made from grain and rice, milk, a bowl, spoon and knife for each child, some different kinds of corn and grain

Eat a bowl of cereal and a piece of bread together. Show the children which type of cereal comes from which kind of grain.

Chat about

Chat about what we do when we wake up in the morning. What kinds of things are made from grain? Which animal gives us milk?

Prayer pocket

Prayer baskets

 Time guide: 5 minutes

You will need: A packet of seeds, an envelope (large enough to hold the packet), the following prayer copied on to medium-weight card (one per child), stickers, coloured crayons, scissors

I plant a seed of prayer for you.

Help the children to seal their envelopes with nothing in them. Cut away the adjacent corners on one of the short ends of the envelope to make a handle. The inside of the envelope now acts as a basket. Decorate and fill with a packet of seeds and the prayer card.

Chat about

Chat about how prayer might help a person to grow. Finish with the following prayer.

Lord, help us to grow day by day,
To be more like you in every way. Amen

Busy box

Farm fun wind chimes

 Time guide: 10 minutes

You will need: Farm-themed biscuit cutters, salt dough (560g plain flour, 140g salt, 375ml warm water), baking trays, string, garden sticks

Help the children to roll out the dough and cut their shapes with the cutters. Poke largish holes in each shape before baking them on a low heat. When cooled, help the children to tie their shapes with string and attach them to garden sticks.

Chat about

Chat about how we can tell when the wind is blowing. How can we tell when God's Spirit is moving?

Home and away link

Send the wind chimes home with the children. 'Home and away' provides a further linked activity.

Go game

Bean game

 Time guide: 5 minutes

You will need: A leader

Instruct the children to form a large circle. Explain that they are all beans. When you say so, they are to begin walking in a clockwise direction. You will call out a type of bean and they are to do the action.

- Runner beans: run round
- Broad beans: walk round with chests out
- String beans: walk holding hands
- Jumping beans: hop round
- Dwarf beans: walk round crouching
- Baked beans: curl up in a ball

Chat about

Chat about beans on toast. Does anyone know how baked beans are made?

Music makers

Farm fun hoe-down

(Tune: Skip to my Lou)

 Time guide: 5 minutes

You will need: A leader and the words below

Divide the group into pairs and sing the song. Do the actions on the first three lines of each verse.

(Flapping wings and pretending to crow)
Roosters on the rooftop—cock a doodle do (x 3)

What will we do, Tom Farmer?

(Linking right arms, then left arms, then right arms again with your partner, and turning in a circle)
Chase them away—shoo, shoo, shoo (x 3)
That's what we'll do, Tom Farmer.

(Pretending to milk a cow)
Cows in the cornfield—moo, moo, moo (x 3)
What will we do, Tom Farmer?

(Linking arms and turning in a circle)
Chase them away—shoo, shoo, shoo (x 3)
That's what we'll do, Tom Farmer.

(Flapping arms and waddling)
Ducks in the dustbin—quack a de do (x 3)
What will we do, Tom Farmer?

(Linking arms and turning in a circle)
Chase them away—shoo, shoo, shoo (x 3)
That's what we'll do, Tom Farmer.

(Wiggling bottom and holding nose)
Pigs in the pantry—poo, poo, poo (x 3)
What will we do, Tom Farmer?

(Linking arms and turning in a circle)
Chase them away—shoo, shoo, shoo (x 3)
That's what we'll do, Tom Farmer.

Chat about

Chat about how many different animal noises there are. How many can the children make in ten seconds? How many different animals can they name in ten seconds?

Memory time

 Time guide: 5 minutes

You will need: The Bible verse 'I planted the seeds… but God made them sprout and grow' (1 Corinthians 3:6)

Teach the children the following actions. Explain that remembering what is said in the Bible can really help us. You are going to try to remember something the Bible says, using both words and actions.

I: Point to self with right index finger.

Planted: Use right hand to pretend to dig in front of you.

The seeds: Touch the fingers of your left hand to your thumb to make a hole and insert the index finger of your right hand into it.

But God: Point up with index finger.

Made: Bunch the fingers of both hands and touch them twice together in the middle.

Them sprout and grow: Move right hand upward from waist height into the sky.

Practise the actions to the verse yourself in advance of the session.

Chat about

Chat about how knowing what the Bible says helps us to grow. How does prayer help us to grow?

2

Home and away

The parable about the growing seeds

Oats, peas, beans and barley grow

Give each child a copy of Home and Away Sheet 2 (see page 75) and a copy of the 'Oats, peas, beans and barley grow' rhyme time poem (see page 85) if desired.

Farmer Friendly's simple deed

Biblical basis: A story about a farmer

A farmer went out to scatter seed in a field… Some of the seeds fell along the road and were stepped on or eaten by birds. Other seeds fell on rocky ground and started growing. But the plants did not have enough water and soon dried up. Some other seeds fell where thorn bushes grew up and choked the plants. The rest of the seeds fell on good ground where they grew and produced a hundred times as many seeds…

This is what the story means: The seed is God's message, and the seeds that fell along the road are the people who hear the message. But the devil comes and snatches the message out of their hearts, so that they will not believe and be saved. The seeds that fell on rocky ground are the people who gladly hear the message and accept it. But they don't have deep roots, and they believe only for a little while. As soon as life gets hard, they give up.

The seeds that fell among the thorn bushes are also people who hear the message. But they are so eager for riches and pleasures that they never produce anything. Those seeds that fell on good ground are the people who listen to the message and keep it in good and honest hearts. They last and produce a harvest.

LUKE 8:5–8, 11–15

Ready, steady, go

- ✪ **Aim:** To affirm that we must prepare the ground as well as plant the seeds
- ✪ **Truth:** God plants his love in our hearts
- ✪ **Themes:** Farming, growing, animals, seeds, seasons and work

In a circle

Name tag crow

 Time guide: **5 minutes**

You will need: A crow name tag for each child (see page 64 for photocopiable template), coloured pens, pencils or crayons, a hole punch, sticky tape, scissors and a length of ribbon

Help the children to cut out and colour their tags and write their names on the front. Place sticky tape toward the top, where you will punch a hole. Loop ribbon through the hole and tie the ends.

Pat-a-pet

Crafty Crow

 Time guide: 5 minutes

You will need: A crow soft toy or puppet

Introduce Crafty Crow to the group as a visitor for the day. Ask the children to pretend to hold seeds in their hands and let the crow eat a bit from each child.

Welcomes and waves

Plant a little seed

Time guide: 5 minutes

You will need: Crafty Crow pat-a-pet, the following rhyme, and a helper to lead

[Name a child] is a little seed in the earth so low.
God sends the rain to help [name] grow.

Instruct the children to curl up like little seeds. When Crafty Crow touches someone on the head, they are to pop up and grow. Repeat the rhyme until all the children have been called. When all the 'seeds' are grown, everyone sits down again.

Story sack

Farmer Friendly's simple deed

 Time guide: 5 minutes

You will need: A brown cloth for the backdrop, a piece of grey fabric for the path, some rocks, a straw hat and red neckerchief, a black glove for your right hand, a pair of green gloves with a bright yellow circle stitched or glued to the palm of the left glove

You will wear: A farmer's outfit: dungarees, shirt, boots, hat and so on

Dress up like a farmer. Hold the story sack in your lap until everyone in the circle is seated and settled. Instruct the children that they are not to move from where they are sitting unless told to do so. Quietly set up the scene.

Remove the hat and put it on your head. Remove the neckerchief and put it around your neck. Remove the brown cloth and lay it out like a rolling field on the floor in front of you. Remove the grey fabric and lay it on one side of the field like a winding path. Remove the rocks and place them in a cluster on the field.

Put the green glove on your left hand and the black glove on your right hand. Keep the black-gloved hand hidden behind your back until needed.

Tell the following rhyme time parable, following the directions in roman (upright) type.

Rhyme time

Farmer Friendly's simple deed

 Time guide: 10 minutes

'Twas Farmer Friendly's simple deed
(Point to yourself with green thumb)
To scatter seed abundantly.
(Pretend to scatter seed on the backdrop with the green-gloved hand)
Some fell where it could not grow,
(Point to path with the green-gloved hand)
Got eaten by a big black crow.
(Bring the black-gloved hand from behind your back, moving it like a crow's beak. Swoop over path and pretend to eat seeds and fly away again out of sight)

Some sprang high in a rocky place,
(Point to the rocks with a green finger. Show the back of the green-gloved hand, wiggling your fingers up in the air like plants)
Was withered by the sun's bright face. (Turn the green-gloved hand around, revealing sun. Wiggle your fingers and bring your hand down as if the plants are wilting)
Some fell among a crowd of weeds
(Show the back of the green-gloved hand. Put the back of the black-gloved hand in the palm of the green hand. Intersperse green and black fingers and wiggle them in the air like plants)
That crushed and choked the growing seeds.
(Roll your fingers in toward the palm of the black-gloved hand. Bring both hands down as if the plants have been choked)

I wonder, do you wonder,
How will Farmer Friendly sow
To help the seeds take root and grow?
(Show both hands. Use the green-gloved hand to remove the black glove and replace it with the other green glove)

She ploughs her field,
(Pretend to dig the brown backdrop with the fingers of both hands)
Pulls out the weeds,
(Pretend to pull stubborn weeds with both hands)
Picks the rocks
(Remove the rocks from the backdrop and place them behind you)
And plants the seeds.
(Pretend to plant seeds carefully on the backdrop)

In good soil the roots take hold;
(Wiggle the fingers of both hands downwards to signify roots)
The crops increase a hundred fold.
(Wiggle your fingers upward and raise your arms in the air)

I wonder, do you wonder,
(Place your right index finger on your chin as if asking a question)
How will we sow
To help God's love take root and grow?
(Place both hands on your heart)

We'll pray a bit,
(Fold your hands in prayer)
We'll talk a bit,
(Move both hands as if they are talking to each other)
We'll make a friend today.
(Clasp hands together as if in friendship)
Bit by bit God's crop will grow.
(Widen the distance between forefinger and thumb of each hand bit by bit)
Away, you crows, away!
(Sweep both hands up and out as if shooing crows away)

Chat about

Chat about what the children liked best about this story. Use some of the following wondering questions:

- ✪ I wonder what kind of seeds the farmer was planting?
- ✪ I wonder what the seed of God's love looks like?
- ✪ I wonder what God's love is like when it grows and grows and grows?
- ✪ I wonder how asking God to help our friends will help them grow?

When you are finished, quietly remove the scene, talking about each item as you return it to the story sack.

Up and about with tickle trunk

 Time guide: 10 minutes

You will need: A large brown sheet (field); grey fabric (path); crumpled brown paper bags (rocks); dungarees, shirt, hat (farmer); black scarf or feather boa (crow); yellow cardboard circle (sun); tractors and other farm toys, green and black gloves

Either encourage the children to play freely with the parable in their own way or choose a cast of children to act out the rhyme time parable.

'We can' can

We can sing 'The farmer plants the seed'

(Tune: The farmer's in his den)

 Time guide: 5 minutes

You will need: A slip of paper that says 'We can sing "The farmer plants the seed"' and the following words

(Rolling arms like a plough)
The farmer ploughs the field,
The farmer ploughs the field,
God helps the seeds to root and grow
The farmer ploughs the field.

The farmer picks the rocks… (Bend over to pick up rocks)
The farmer plants the seeds… (Pretend to scatter seeds)
The farmer pulls the weeds… (Pretend to pull weeds)
The sun begins to shine… (Make a circle with arms)
The rain begins to fall… (Wiggle fingers in downward motion)
The seeds begin to grow… (Crouch and begin to grow)
The roots grow deep and strong… (Stamp feet)
The leaves grow straight and tall… (Stretch arms high)
We all have food to eat… (Pretend to eat)

Choose a child to remove the instructions from the 'We can' can. Sing the song and do the actions as a group.

Chat about

Chat about the seeds in the story that fell and grew in good soil. Have the children ever watched a farmer at work in the field? How does being kind to one another help us grow?

Food fun

Apple shake-ups

 Time guide: 10 minutes

You will need: Apples, knife, sugar, cinnamon, a spoon and a plastic sandwich bag for each child

Peel and slice one apple per child before the session. Help the children to work in pairs. Place one to two tablespoons of sugar and half a teaspoon of cinnamon into each plastic sandwich bag. Put a few pieces of apple into the bag and shake it until the apple pieces are coated. Take them out and eat them.

Chat about

Chat about the fact that some of the seeds in the story were choked and crushed by weeds. Talk about the kind of things that worry the children. How does being friends with Jesus help us to worry less?

Prayer pocket

Wordless prayer book

 Time guide: 5 minutes

You will need: A prayer pocket decorated like an apple, one set of apple cards (grey, red, white, gold, green) stapled at the top corners for each child (see photocopiable template on page 70)

Put the wordless books into the prayer pocket before the session. Remind the children about the farmer who planted the seed. Explain that in just the same way, God plants his love in our hearts. Remove one of the wordless books from the prayer pocket. Show the children how to use it to share God's love.

- ✪ Grey apple page: We all do wrong things.
- ✪ Red apple page: Jesus loves us.
- ✪ White apple page: God forgives us.
- ✪ Gold apple page: God plants his seed of love in our hearts.
- ✪ Green apple page: We grow to be like Jesus.

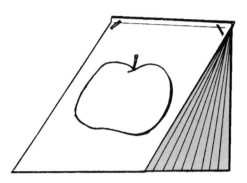

Chat about

Chat about some of the wrong things people do. How does Jesus show us that he loves us? How does God show us that he forgives us? How do we show that God has planted his seed of love in our hearts? What are some ways that we can be like Jesus?

Finish with the following prayer.

Lord God, thank you that your love is found
In our hearts and all around. Amen

Home and away link

Send the wordless prayer book home with each child. 'Home and away' provides a further linked activity.

Busy box

Crafty crow puppet

 Time guide: 10 minutes

You will need: Thick black card, yellow tissue paper, scissors, PVA glue, sticky tape, white card and a black felt-tipped pen to make two card eyes for each puppet, thick card

Make a triangle template out of card with a base of approximately 18cm and sides of approximately 20cm. Help the children to cut six equal-sized triangles from the black card. Form a pyramid by taping three triangles together up the sides. Form another pyramid by taping the other three triangles together up the sides.

To form the pointy head of the crow, tape the two pyramids together along one of the base edges, so that the fingers and thumb can be inserted into the two halves to open and close the 'beak'. To decorate the beak, help the children tear the yellow tissue paper up into bits and glue the pieces collage-fashion up from the points of both pyramids. Make sure to leave at least the top third of the puppet black. Glue a pair of card eyes toward the top.

To make the puppet easier to use, attach a 10cm strip of thick card to the inside of each pyramid. Tape the strips at each end to stop the hand slipping out when opening and closing the crow's beak.

Chat about

Chat about how some of the seeds in the story were stolen by a crow. What sort of things stop us from being kind to one another? What sort of things stop us from being happy with what we have?

Go game

Crows in the cornfield

 Time guide: 5 minutes

You will need: A person to be the scarecrow, a person to be the crow, a beanbag to be the packet of 'seeds'.

Ask the children to make a big circle and sit down facing the middle. Explain that they are all crows sitting in their nests and that the inside of the circle is a cornfield. A 'scarecrow' will be chosen to stand in the middle with arms out, legs crossed and eyes closed. A packet of seeds (beanbag) will be placed on the floor behind the scarecrow. The leader will silently point to a crow to begin the game.

The crow must sneak up and steal the seeds from the scarecrow. As soon as the crow lifts the seeds, the other crows in the circle shout 'Crows in the cornfield!' The crow must then run around the outside of the circle, flapping its wings, until it is sitting safe in its nest again without being tagged by the scarecrow. Choose a new scarecrow and crow and play again.

Music makers

Dingle-dangle scarecrow

 Time guide: 5 minutes

You will need: A set of shakers and ankle bells for each child, and the following words.

When all the cows were sleeping, and the sun had gone to bed.
Up jumped the scarecrow, and this is what he said:

I'm a dingle-dangle scarecrow with a flippy-floppy hat (Children jump up from crouched position)
I can shake my hands like this, (Shake shakers)
I can shake my feet like that! (Shake ankle bells)

When all the hens were roosting, with the moon behind a cloud,
Up jumped the scarecrow, and shouted very loud:

I'm a dingle-dangle scarecrow…

When the dogs were in the kennel, and the doves were in the loft,
Up jumped the scarecrow and whispered very soft:

I'm a dingle-dangle scarecrow…

Give each child a set of shakers to hold and a set of jingle bells to put around their ankles. Instruct them to crouch down as low as they can. Explain that they are scarecrows and that they are to keep their instruments quiet until it is time to jump up and sing, 'I can shake my hands like this, I can shake my feet like that.' Have a practice, then sing the whole song through.

Chat about

Chat about why farmers make scarecrows.

Memory time

 Time guide: 5 minutes

You will need: The Bible verse 'Look to God and believe the good news!' (Mark 1:15, paraphrased).

Teach the children the following actions. Explain that remembering what is said in the Bible can really help us, and that they are going to try to remember something the Bible says, using both words and actions.

Look: Point to right eye with right finger.

To God: Point up to God.

And believe: Chop palm of left hand once with edge of right hand.

The good news: Make the sign for Jesus: touch the middle finger of your right hand to the palm of your left and vice versa.

Practise the actions of the verse yourself in advance of the session.

Chat about

Chat about what the Bible means by good news. See if the children can remember the wordless prayer book (see page 25).

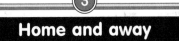
Home and away

Give each child a copy of Home and Away Sheet 3 (see page 76) and a copy of the 'Farmer Friendly's simple deed' rhyme time poem (see page 86) if desired.

Good Sammy

Biblical basis: The good Samaritan

As a man was going down from Jerusalem to Jericho, robbers attacked him and grabbed everything he had. They beat him up and ran off, leaving him half dead.

A priest happened to be going down the same road. But when he saw the man, he walked by on the other side. Later a temple helper came to the same place. But when he saw the man who had been beaten up, he also went by on the other side.

A man from Samaria then came travelling along that road. When he saw the man, he felt sorry for him and went over to him. He treated his wounds with olive oil and wine and bandaged them. Then he put him on his own donkey and took him to an inn, where he took care of him. The next morning he gave the innkeeper two silver coins and said, 'Please take care of the man. If you spend more than this on him, I will pay you when I return.'

Then Jesus asked, 'Which one of these three people was a real neighbour to the man who was beaten up by robbers?'

The teacher answered, 'The one who showed pity.'

Jesus said, 'Go and do the same!'

LUKE 10:30–37

Ready, steady, go

- ✪ **Aim:** To affirm that God loves everyone and asks us to do the same
- ✪ **Truth:** God wants us to help others and treat them kindly
- ✪ **Themes:** Caring, travel, our bodies and helping

In a circle

Name tag donkey

 Time guide: 5 minutes

You will need: A donkey name tag for each child (see page 64 for photocopiable template), coloured pens, pencils or crayons, a hole punch, sticky tape, scissors and a length of ribbon.

Help the children to cut out and colour their tags and write their names on the front. Place sticky tape toward the top, where you will punch a hole. Loop ribbon through the hole and tie the ends.

Pat-a-pet

Dinky Donkey

 Time guide: 5 minutes

You will need: A donkey soft toy or puppet

Introduce Dinky Donkey to the group as a visitor for the day. Get the children to welcome Dinky Donkey by pretending their hands are donkey ears and saying 'Hee-haw, hee-haw.' Talk about how donkeys used to help people travel when there were no cars.

Welcomes and waves

What can we do?

 Time guide: 5 minutes

You will need: Dinky Donkey pat-a-pet, the following chant, and a helper to lead.

Every time

[Name two children], what can you do
With the [name a body part] that God gave you?

Last time, with pat-a-pet

Dinky Donkey, what can you do
With the body that God gave you?
(Donkey kicks high in the air, braying loudly)

Instruct the children to stay seated until their names are called. When their name is heard, they are to stand up and do an action related to the body part mentioned, then sit down again. Body parts and examples of actions may include:

- ✪ Feet *(stamp, walk, run, tap or stand)*
- ✪ Hands *(wave, clap, shake or pray)*
- ✪ Fingers *(wiggle, pull, or pretend to pick something up)*
- ✪ Arms *(fold, reach high, hug, stretch out like an aeroplane, or move in a circle)*
- ✪ Elbows *(bend to move arm or to lean head in hands)*
- ✪ Eyes *(blink, wink, peep or cry)*
- ✪ Nose *(breathe, sniff, smell or sneeze)*
- ✪ Ears *(wiggle, listen or hear)*
- ✪ Mouth *(eat, talk, shout, sing, whisper or blow a kiss)*
- ✪ Knees *(bend to move lower leg or kneel down)*
- ✪ Toes *(wiggle, stand on tiptoe or walk)*
- ✪ Legs *(run, jump, skip or kick)*

Story sack

Good Sammy

 Time guide: 5 minutes

You will need: A set of Good Sammy stick puppets (see photocopiable template sheet on page 65) as follows: a crooked man, a robber, a Busy Bob, a Wallace, a Good Sammy, a nurse. (See instructions below)

You will wear: A cowboy hat, vest and star

Photocopy the puppet templates on to medium-weight card, colour and cut out. Stick each puppet on to a craft stick and place in the story sack. Dress like a cowboy. Hold the story sack in your lap until everyone in the circle is seated and settled. Instruct the children that they are not to move from where they are sitting unless told to do so. Quietly remove the stick puppets from the sack.

Tell the following rhyme time parable, following the directions in roman (upright) type.

Rhyme time

Good Sammy

 Time guide: 10 minutes

There was a crooked man
Who walked a crooked mile,
(Walk the crooked man puppet along a pretend road, up a hill)
Then a robber robbed him
And took away his smile!
(The robber puppet knocks over the crooked man and runs away)

Busy Bob bobbed along
But busied right on by.
(Busy Bob puppet drives by in his fancy car)
Wallace wouldn't help,
Wouldn't even try.
(Wallace puppet rides by on his scooter)

I wonder, do you wonder,
Will anybody care?
Look! Here comes Good Sammy.
He's helping with a prayer.
(Good Sammy puppet comes along on his hobby horse)

He takes the man to hospital
Where he'll get much better,

(Good Sammy takes the crooked man to the nurse puppet and rides off)
Giving him some flowers
And a get-well letter.
(Nurse pretends to put crooked man on a bed and cover him up)

I wonder, do you wonder,
Who was a friend today?
(Good Sammy returns to see his new friend)
Three cheers for Good Sammy:
Hooray! Hooray! Hooray!

Chat about

Chat about what the children liked best about this story. Use some of the following wondering questions:

- ✪ I wonder if the crooked man has a name?
- ✪ I wonder why the robber wanted the crooked man's money?
- ✪ I wonder how Busy Bob and Wallace felt as they went by?
- ✪ I wonder how the crooked man felt when Busy Bob and Wallace left him?
- ✪ I wonder why Good Sammy stopped to help?
- ✪ I wonder if you have ever needed help?
- ✪ I wonder what you do when you see people who need help?

When you are finished, quietly remove the scene, talking about each puppet as you return it to the story sack.

Home and away link

Send a sheet of Good Sammy stick puppet templates home with each child. 'Home and away' provides a further linked activity.

Up and about with tickle trunk

 Time guide: 10 minutes

You will need: Backpack, walking stick and hiking boots (crooked man); a nurse and doctor outfit and first aid kit; a vest, cowboy hat and hobby horse (Good Sammy); a business suit, tie, briefcase (Busy Bob); skating gear (Wallace); a robber outfit and inflatable hammer, toy steering wheel or ride-in car

Either encourage the children to play freely with the parable in their own way or choose a cast of children to act out the rhyme time parable.

'We can' can

We can be Dinky Donkeys

 Time guide: 5 minutes

You will need: A slip of paper that says, 'We can be Dinky Donkeys' and the following words

I'm a Dinky Donkey (fingers up for ears)
Walking very slow. (walk slowly)
Now I'm walking faster, (walk faster)
I'm running, watch me go! (start to run)
I'm kicking way up high, (kick high)
I'm kicking way down low. (kick low)
Hee haw! Hee-haw! (bray and throw head back)
Just watch me go!

Choose a child to remove the instructions from the 'We can' can. Do the chant and actions together.

Chat about

Chat about whether the children have ever ridden a donkey or a horse. How many ways of travelling can they think of (boat, car, plane, bike and so on)?

Food fun

Ginger Sammies

 Time guide: 10 minutes

You will need: At least one pre-made gingerbread man and plastic knife per child, icing and other decorations: different coloured icing pens, sprinkles, chocolate chips and so on

Help the children to decorate their Good Sammy gingerbread man. Eat up and clean up.

Chat about

Chat about why Busy Bob was in such a hurry. Have any of the children ever been too busy to help? Why was Good Sammy so helpful? Can anyone remember a time when they were helpful?

Prayer pocket

Taking care of others

 Time guide: 5 minutes

You will need: A prayer pocket decorated like a first aid kit, magazine pictures of people in caring professions, such as nurses, doctors, teachers, fire fighters, first aiders, foreign aid workers and so on

Put the pictures in the prayer pocket before the session. Choose a few children to help you. Remove one picture at a time. Talk about what the person in the picture does for a job and who they take care of or help.

Chat about

Chat about whether the children know anyone who does this kind of job. Can anyone tell about a time they needed help from the doctor or nurse? What would happen if these people didn't help others? How can we ask God to help people who help others?

Finish with the following prayer.

Thank you, Lord God, for the people who take care of others.
Help them to be brave and strong.
Help us to help others, too. Amen

Busy box

Whose shoes?

 Time guide: 10 minutes

You will need: Several pairs of different kinds of shoes, such as ballet shoes, garden boots, trainers, roller boots, school shoes, worn out shoes, or football boots, with different patterned soles; also a set of horseshoes, coloured crayons, scissors and plain paper

Place the paper over the soles and horseshoes and use the crayons to make a rubbing of them. Trace and cut around the rubbings to make footprints. Keep the rubbings aside for use with the 'Music makers' activity below.

Chat about

Chat about who might wear these shoes. Where might the person wearing these shoes go in them? How might they need help? Who might be their friends? How would you want someone to treat you if you were in these shoes?

Go game

Rope relay

 Time guide: 5 minutes

You will need: A long length of rope and a backpack for each team

Divide the children into teams and ask them to sit down in lines. Lay a rope out in a gentle squiggle in front of each group. Each child is to wear the backpack, walk along the road (rope) and back and pass the backpack on to the next child. The quickest team wins. Play the game several times, changing the method—for example:

- ✪ Jump from side to side along the rope
- ✪ Bunny hop over the rope
- ✪ Walk with one foot on either side of the rope
- ✪ Hop along the rope on one foot
- ✪ Crawl along the rope
- ✪ Move along the rope using one hand and one foot

Chat about

Chat about a journey the children have taken.

Music makers

Horseshoe shuffle

 Time guide: 5 minutes

You will need: The shoe prints and set of horseshoe prints you made under 'Busy box', Blu-tack, a CD of country and western music, CD player

Blu-tack to the floor one set of horseshoe prints and enough pairs of shoe prints so that every child can participate around the room. Play some country and western music. When the music stops, the children must find and stand on a pair of prints. Whoever is left standing on the horseshoe prints must bray, nay and kick like a donkey. Play several times.

Chat about

Chat about how can we stop what we are doing and help others.

Memory time

 Time guide: 5 minutes

You will need: The Bible verse 'Treat others as you want them to treat you' (Matthew 7:12)

Teach the children the following actions. Explain that remembering what is said in the Bible can really help us, and that they are going to try to remember something Jesus said, using both words and actions.

Treat others: Hug yourself, then sweep your right hand out in front of you from left to right, palm up.

As you want them to treat you: Hug yourself, then point to self.

Practise the actions to the verse yourself in advance of the session.

Chat about

Chat about how the children would want to be treated if:

✪ They fell and hurt their knee.
✪ Someone wouldn't play with them.
✪ They were lonely, afraid or worried.
✪ They were in hospital.

4

Home and away

Give each child a copy of Home and Away Sheet 4 (see page 77) and a copy of the 'Good Sammy' rhyme time poem (see page 87) if desired, plus a copy of the Good Sammy stick puppets templates (see page 65).

Grandma Guddle's Muddle

Ready, steady, go

- ✪ **Aim:** To affirm how precious and valuable we are to God
- ✪ **Truth:** We are precious to God and he will not forget about us
- ✪ **Themes:** Counting, emotions, memory, lost and found, animals and work

Biblical basis: One coin

What will a woman do if she has ten silver coins and loses one of them? Won't she light a lamp, sweep the floor, and look carefully until she finds it? Then she will call in her friends and neighbours and say, 'Let's celebrate! I've found the coin I lost.' Jesus said, 'In the same way God's angels are happy when even one person turns to him.'

LUKE 15:8–10

In a circle

Name tag cat

 Time guide: 5 minutes

You will need: A cat name tag for each child (see page 64 for photocopiable template), coloured pens, pencils or crayons, a hole punch, sticky tape, scissors and a length of ribbon.

Help the children to cut out and colour their tags and write their names on the front. Place sticky tape toward the top, where you will punch a hole. Loop ribbon through the hole and tie the ends.

Pat-a-pet

Bitty Kitty

 Time guide: 5 minutes

You will need: A cat soft toy or puppet

Introduce Bitty Kitty to the group as a visitor for the day. Ask the children to cup their hands as if they are holding a saucer of milk. Bring Bitty Kitty around the circle to sip milk from each hand.

Welcomes and waves

Grandma's washing

 Time guide: 5 minutes

You will need: Bitty Kitty pat-a-pet, the following rhyme and a helper to lead

Grandma's washing, Grandma's washing,
Rub, rub, rub; rub, rub, rub.
(Pretend to wash clothes)
Picked up [child's] [item of clothing]
And threw it in the tub.
(Pretend to throw item of clothing in tub)

Last time
Grandma's washing, Grandma's washing,
Rub, rub, rub; rub, rub, rub.
(Pretend to wash clothes)
Run, Bitty Kitty; run, Bitty Kitty
Before she throws you in the tub!

Repeat the rhyme adding a different child's name and item of clothing with description each time: blue socks, pink trousers, yellow T-shirt, fluffy hairband, black shoes and so on. Make sure you include Bitty Kitty in the fun.

Story sack

Grandma Guddle's muddle

 Time guide: 5 minutes

You will need: A handbag large enough to contain a Grandma Guddle puppet or doll with an unseen penny in her pocket, Bitty Kitty pat-a-pet, a hankie, nine pennies in a coin purse, a plastic magnifying glass, a toy brush and dust pan, a small rug, a large pair of knickers, a duster, a torch, a mobile phone, a toy teapot, cup and saucer

You will wear: A shawl and granny bonnet

Dress like a granny. Hold the story sack in your lap until everyone in the circle is seated and settled. Instruct the children that they are not to move from where they are sitting unless told to do so. Quietly set up the scene.

Remove the handbag from the story sack. Explain that this is no ordinary handbag. Someone lives in this handbag! Ask the children if they know anyone who lives in a handbag. Ask the children if they would like to see who lives in the handbag. Open the clasp and remove Grandma Guddle. Introduce her to the children.

Tell the following rhyme time parable, following the directions in roman (upright) type.

Rhyme time

Grandma Guddle's muddle

 Time guide: 10 minutes

Old Grandma Guddle is in such a muddle
And doesn't know what to do!
(Granny starts digging around in her handbag)
'Oh dear,' says she, 'I greatly fear
That I have lost my penny.'
(Puts hands to head and shakes it)

What? Lost your penny? You poor old Granny!
Then she began to cry.
(Granny removes hankie from handbag and begins to cry)
'Boo hoo, boo hoo, boo hoo, boo hoo.'
Then she began to cry.
(Granny blows her nose and tosses the hankie aside)

'I once had ten but when I looked again
I couldn't find the one.'
(Granny removes the coin purse from the handbag)
I wonder, do you wonder,
Where has Granny's penny gone?
(Open coin purse, pretend to count, then set it aside)

'I'll look,' says Granny, 'in every cranny!'
Then she began to spy.
(Granny removes magnifying glass from handbag and begins to look)
'I spy, I spy, with my little eye.'
Then she began to spy.
(Granny tosses the magnifying glass aside)

She lifts the cat,
(Granny removes Bitty Kitty from the handbag and sets her aside)
Looks under the mat,
(Granny removes the rug from the handbag and tosses aside)

Sweeps the floor with a broom.
(Granny removes the brush and dustpan from the
handbag, pretends to sweep, then tosses them aside)
Washes, dusts and polishes
(Granny removes a large pair of knickers and a duster
from the handbag, then tosses them aside)
In each corner of every room.
(Granny removes a torch from the handbag and
shines it around the children)

'It's uncanny,' says Granny. 'Where is my penny,
Oh where, oh where have I put it?
(Granny sets the torch aside and taps her pocket)
'Oh dear,' says she, 'see here, see here!
I've found it in my pocket!'
(Granny giggles and removes the hidden penny from
her apron pocket)

What? Found your penny? Hooray for Granny!
We all begin to cheer!
(Lead the children in the following cheer)
Hooray, hooray, hooray, hurrah!
We all begin to cheer!

Old Grandma Guddle gives Kitty a cuddle,
(Granny gives Bitty Kitty a cuddle and then pours a
cup of tea out of the handbag)
Then phones a friend to say,
(Granny takes a mobile phone out of her handbag and
pretends to talk to her friend)
'I lost my penny, but now I have found it!
Oh what a busy day!'

I wonder, do you wonder,
Does God find us near or far?
Even when we think we're lost
He remembers where we are.

Chat about

Chat about what the children liked best about this story.
Use some of the following wondering questions:

- ✪ I wonder how it feels to lose something special and
  find it again?
- ✪ I wonder what things are special for you?
- ✪ I wonder if you have ever forgotten where you put
  something special?
- ✪ I wonder what is most special to God?
- ✪ I wonder if God ever forgets about his special
  things?

When you are finished, quietly remove the scene,
including Grandma Guddle, talking about each item as
you return it to the story sack.

Up and about with tickle trunk

 Time guide: 10 minutes

You will need: A Grandma Guddle outfit, old
handbags, play money and coin purses, objects
for playing house, such as toy pots, pans,
vacuum cleaner, broom, clothes basket, tea set,
dusters, ironing board, iron, phone and so on

Either encourage the children to play freely with the
parable in their own way or choose a cast of children to
act out the rhyme time parable.

'We can' can

We can play 'Grandma Guddle, may I?'

 Time guide: 5 minutes

You will need: A slip of paper that says, 'We
can play "Grandma Guddle, may I?"' and the
following instructions.

- ✪ Sweep the floor
- ✪ Cuddle Bitty Kitty
- ✪ Dust the stairs
- ✪ Touch your nose
- ✪ Take a nap
- ✪ Jump up and down
- ✪ Turn around
- ✪ Wiggle your hips
- ✪ Have a cup of tea
- ✪ Turn around in a circle
- ✪ Hop on one leg
- ✪ Wave your arms

Choose a child to remove the instructions from the 'We
can' can. The leader pretends to be Grandma Guddle
and calls out the instructions one at a time. After each
instruction, the children ask, 'Grandma Guddle, may I?'
If Grandma Guddle says, 'Yes, you may', the children
do the action as instructed. If Grandma Guddle says,
'No, you may not', the children do not do as instructed.

Chat about

Chat about what the children like to do when they visit
their grandparents.

Food fun

Hide and seek cakes

 Time guide: 10 minutes

You will need: A fairy cake, muffin and chocolate coin per child, a coin purse with ten coins in it

Before the session begins, carefully cut off the top of the fairy cake or muffin and hollow it out. Fill with a chocolate coin and put the top back on. Eat the cakes together. Use the coins in the purse in 'Chat about' below.

Chat about

Use the coins in the purse to count up to ten together and do simple sums while you are eating.

Prayer pocket

Drop the penny

 Time guide: 5 minutes

You will need: A large open-mouthed jar and a prayer pocket, decorated like a coin and containing several items that will make a noise when dropped into the jar, such as a clothes peg, a penny, a comb, a marble, a pencil and a pin

Remove an item from the prayer pocket and ask the children to listen carefully as you drop it into the jar. Do this for every item. Now, do it again without the children looking. Ask them to guess what item has been dropped just by the sound it makes.

Chat about

Chat about whether God knows what we sound like. How can we listen to God?

Finish with the following prayer.

Lord God,
You remember me,
You remember me,
Help me to remember you
As you remember me. Amen

Busy box

Grandma's memory book

 Time guide: 10 minutes

You will need: Purse template (see photocopiable sheet on page 68), coloured card, plain paper, scissors, paper, stapler, PVA glue, coloured pens, stickers

Photocopy the purse template, ten on to plain paper and two on to coloured card. Staple the plain purses together between the coloured purses to make a memory book. Use the pens and stickers to decorate the cover.

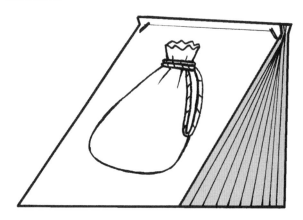

Chat about

Chat about what the children like best about their grandmas. What fun things have they done together?

Home and away link

Send the memory book home with each child. 'Home and away' provides a further linked activity.

Go game

Handbag hunt

 Time guide: 5 minutes

You will need: A large handbag, a packet of hankies, sweets, hairpins, a toy train, a toy car, a teddy, crayons, notepad, pen, a large pair of knickers, a book, reading glasses, a coin purse, a pair of gloves, a mobile phone, a rain cap, an orange, a torch, a library card, a hairbrush and a silver coin

Hide all the items (except the handbag and the coin) around the room before the children arrive. When it is time to play, show the children the empty handbag and read out the list of items to be found. Put the items in the handbag as the children find them. When it is certain that the coin can't be found, gather everyone together. Pretend to look among the children for it. Keep the coin hidden out of sight and produce it from behind a child's ear in a 'sleight of hand'. If time permits, see how many items the children can remember.

Chat about
Chat about bags or backpacks that the children have. What do they carry in their bags or backpacks?

Music makers

Musical clusters

 Time guide: 5 minutes

You will need: A drum

Explain to the children that you are going to beat the drum. They are to listen and count the beats aloud as a group. When you have finished on the drum, they are to quickly form groups of the same number of beats. For example, if you beat the drum five times, they are to find some others and make a group of five. If you beat the drum twice, they are to find someone else and make a group of two.

Chat about
Chat about how many coins Grandma Guddle had altogether.

Memory time

 Time guide: 5 minutes

You will need: The Bible verse 'God will never forget you' (Isaiah 49:15b, paraphrased)

Teach the children the following actions. Explain that remembering what is said in the Bible can really help us, and that they are going to try to remember something the Bible says, using both words and actions.

God: Point up to God.
Will never: Shake head and hands as if saying 'no'.
Forget: Tap temple once with right hand.
You: Sweep outwards from left to right with your right hand, palm open and facing upward.

Practise the actions to the verse yourself in advance of the session.

Chat about
Chat about getting lost and found.

Home and away

Give each child a copy of Home and Away Sheet 5 (see page 78) and a copy of the 'Grandma Guddle's muddle' rhyme time poem (see page 88) if desired.

Mick and Mac

Ready, steady, go

- **Aim:** To show the wisdom of listening to Jesus
- **Truth:** We will be strong inside if we listen to Jesus and do what he says
- **Themes:** Building, listening, weather and work

Biblical basis: The two builders

Jesus said: 'Anyone who comes and listens to me and obeys me is like someone who dug down deep and built a house on solid rock. When the flood came and the river rushed against the house, it was built so well that it didn't even shake. But anyone who hears what I say and doesn't obey me is like someone whose house wasn't built on solid rock. As soon as the river rushed against that house, it was smashed to pieces!'

LUKE 6:47–49

In a circle

Name tag dog

 Time guide: 5 minutes

You will need: A dog name tag for each child (see page 64 for photocopiable template), coloured pens, pencils or crayons, a hole punch, sticky tape, scissors and a length of ribbon.

Help the children to cut out and colour their tags and write their names on the front. Place sticky tape toward the top, where you will punch a hole. Loop ribbon through the hole and tie the ends.

Pat-a-pet

Digger Dog

Time guide: 5 minutes

You will need: A dog soft toy or puppet

Introduce Digger Dog to the group as a visitor for the day. Ask if any of the children have a dog at home. Talk about what they like to do with their dogs.

Welcomes and waves

Digger Dog, what did you do?

Time guide: 5 minutes

You will need: Digger Dog pat-a-pet, the following chant, and a helper to lead

Children: *Digger Dog, Digger Dog, what did you do?*
Child holding Digger: *Woof, woof, woof!*
    I buried… (child names an object)

Explain that Digger Dog belongs to a builder. He likes to dig holes and bury things. Pass Digger Dog to each child in turn. Lead the children in the chant, allowing each child to choose an object to fill in the gap. Continue until all the children have had a turn holding Digger Dog.

Objects could include boots, hammer, measuring tape, goggles, hard hat, ladder, plans, drill, shovel, bucket, screwdriver, saw, lunchbox and so on.

Story sack

Mick and Mac

 Time guide: 5 minutes

You will need: A play figure dressed as a builder (Mick); a play figure dressed in beach clothes (Mac); a house made of interlocking bricks (Lego or similar); a shack loosely made of craft sticks; an assortment of instruments: cymbals, shakers, drums and so on

You will wear: A builder's outfit (hard hat, boots and tool belt)

Hold the story sack in your lap until everyone in the circle is seated and settled. Instruct the children that they are not to move from where they are sitting unless told to do so.

Remove the instruments and place them in front of you. Explain that you will need help during the story to make a big crashing sound. Tell the children that a helper will come to them where they are in the circle and give them an instrument. They are to hold the instruments quietly until you tell them what to do. Have a few practices making a big crashing noise and stopping suddenly.

Tell the following rhyme time parable, following the directions in roman (upright) type.

Rhyme time

Mick and Mac

 Time guide: 10 minutes

Mick is a builder,
(Remove Mick and place him to the right)

Mac is too.
(Remove Mac and place him to the left)
Building houses is what they do.
(Tap your hard hat twice and nod)

Mick is wise,
(Point to Mick)
His plan is sound:
(Remove and show house plan and set it aside)
To build a house on solid ground.
(Tap your hard hat twice)

Mick is thoughtful,
(Point to Mick),
Knows the trick,
Lays a foundation brick by brick.
(Remove brick house and put it beside Mick)

Mac is hapless,
(Point to Mac and roll your eyes)
Has no plan,
(Shake head)
Decides to build on sandy land.
(Tap hard hat twice)

Mac is foolish,
(Point to Mac and shake head sadly)
Mac is thick,
Builds his shack quick, quick, quick.
(Tap hard hat three times. Remove shack and put it beside Mac)

Mick is happy,
(Point to Mick and smile)
Mac is too
(Point to Mac and smile)
Until a storm begins to brew.
(Hug yourself and shiver, looking up at the sky)

I wonder, do you wonder,
Whether the weather will win?
(Hand out as if testing for rain)
Will Mac's shack come crashing in?
(Point to Mac's shack)

Walls do wobble,
(Wobble the shack a bit)
Doors do creak,
(Accent the word 'creak')
'Eek,' says Mac, 'I've sprung a leak!'
(Mac jumps up and down in a mad panic)

Mumble, rumble,
Flash, boom, bash
(Children make noise on their instruments until you quieten them)

Mac's shack crumbles, crash, crash, crash!
(Squash Mac's shack with your hand)

'Sorry Mac, mate,'
(Bring Mick over to Mac)
Says Mick to his friend.
'Come and stay with me till the storm's at an end.'
(Move Mick and Mac to Mick's house and stand them together)

I wonder, do you wonder,
How will we win
When our worries come crashing in?
(Wobble your body)

We'll ask Jesus
What's in God's plan.
When the storm hits us he'll help us stand.
(Sit upright and sturdy)

Chat about

Chat about what the children liked best about this story. Use some of the following wondering questions:

- ✪ I wonder why it is important to have a plan?
- ✪ I wonder how Mick felt in his house during the storm?
- ✪ I wonder how Mac felt when his shack fell down?
- ✪ I wonder what makes you feel wobbly inside?
- ✪ I wonder how we can find out what's in God's plan?
- ✪ I wonder how knowing that God has a plan can help us be strong?

When you are finished, quietly remove the scene, talking about each item as you return it to the story sack.

Up and about with tickle trunk

 Time guide: 10 minutes

You will need: Play tools: hammers, saws, drills, measuring tapes, screwdrivers and so on; builders' dressing-up clothes: hard hat, goggles, boots, tool belt and so on; building bricks, blocks or shoeboxes; storm noises: drums, cymbals and shakers

Either encourage the children to play freely with the parable in their own way or choose a cast of children to act out the rhyme time parable.

'We can' can

We can play 'Mick says'

 Time guide: 5 minutes

You will need: A leader to lead and the following commands.

Mick says put on your goggles.
Mick says put on your hard hat.
Mick says put on your tool belt.
Mac says put on your sunglasses.
Mick says put on your boots.
Mac says take your boots off.
Mac says put on your sunhat.
Mick says look at the plan.
Mac says read a comic.
Mick says dig the foundation.
Mac says dig with a toy spade.
Mick says mix the concrete.
Mick says pour the concrete.
Mac says pour a cold drink.
Mick says measure.
Mick says climb the ladder.
Mac says fall off the ladder.
Mac says put on your sun cream.
Mick says saw.
Mick says hammer.
Mac says drop the hammer on your toe.
Mick says drill.
Mick says paint.
Mick says sit down and take a break.

The leader calls out the commands. The children are to do what Mick says but not what Mac says.

Chat about

Chat about a time when the children saw builders working on a house. Talk about what it's like to build a sandcastle.

Food fun

Rice Krispie bricks

 Time guide: 10 minutes

You will need: 125g Rice Krispies, 40 large marshmallows, 4g butter or margarine, Swiss roll tin, greaseproof paper

Melt the butter or margarine in a pan, add the marshmallows and stir until sticky over a low heat. Remove from the heat and add the Rice Krispies. Press mixture into a Swiss roll tin, lined with greaseproof paper, and allow to set before cutting into bricks. Display in the form of a brick house. Eat up and clean up.

Prayer pocket

Card houses and prayer bricks

 Time guide: 5 minutes

You will need: A prayer pocket, a house shape and four prayer bricks for each child, copied on to card (see photocopiable sheet on page 71), crayons, scissors, sticky tape

Help the children to colour their houses and tape them to the front of the prayer pocket. Cut out the prayer bricks and put them in the pocket (Kitchen: Thank you for my food; Bedroom: Thank you for my bed; Living room: Thank you for my family; Door: Thank you for my friends)

Chat about
Chat about the children's homes. What do they like about their homes? What do they like about the people who live in their homes?

Home and away link
Send the card houses and prayer bricks home with each child. 'Home and away' provides a further linked activity.

Busy box

Rain shakers

 Time guide: 10 minutes

You will need: A clean crisps can with lid for each child, sticky tape, dry beans, PVA glue, scissors, paper, stickers, tinsel, weather themed pictures to decorate

Help the children to decorate their rain shakers in a weather theme. Add some beans to each can and put the lids on. Put tape around the lids to keep the beans in, and set aside to dry. Use for the 'Music makers' activity (see below).

Chat about
Chat about what the children like to do on rainy days. What do they like to do on sunny days?

Go game

Sandbox scavenge

 Time guide: 5 minutes

You will need: A sandbox with the following things hidden in it: bucket, spade, sun tan lotion, sunglasses, watering can, swimming trunks, plans for a sandcastle, hammer, measuring tape, a small bag of nails, saw, drill, plans for a brick house, hard hat and goggles

Divide the group into two teams. When you blow the whistle, the first person from each team is to run to the sandbox, find an item that would be used to build a brick house and bring it back to the team. Continue the game until each person in the team has had a turn or all the items have been found.

Chat about
Chat about how the things that you found to build a house are used.

Music makers

I hear thunder

(Tune: Frère Jacques)

 Time guide: 5 minutes

You will need: Rain shakers (see above), words and directions below.

I hear thunder, I hear thunder.
(Tap the lid of the rain shaker)
Hark, don't you? Hark, don't you?
(Pretend to listen)
Pitter patter raindrops, pitter patter raindrops
(Shake rain shakers)
I'm wet through, (shiver) *so are you.*
(Point to each other)

I see blue skies, I see blue skies
(Shade eyes and look up)
Way up high, way up high.
(Reach up with arms)
Hurry up the sunshine, hurry up the sunshine,
(Shiver)
We'll soon dry, we'll soon dry.
(Rub arms and legs)

Sing the song together using the rain shakers.

Chat about

Chat about how storms make us feel. What do the children like or not like about walking in the rain? How can we listen to Jesus?

Memory time

 Time guide: **5 minutes**

You will need: The Bible verse 'Don't be worried. Have faith in Jesus' (John 14:1, paraphrased)

Teach the children the following actions. Explain that remembering what is said in the Bible can really help us, and that they are going to try to remember something the Bible says, using both words and actions.

Don't be worried: Shake head and pretend to chew fingernails.
Have faith: Right thumb to temple.
In Jesus: Touch middle finger of right hand to palm of left and vice versa.

Practise the actions to the verse yourself in advance of the session.

Chat about

Chat about what it means to have faith in Jesus.

Home and away

Give each child a copy of Home and Away Sheet 6 (see page 79) and a copy of the 'Mick and Mac' rhyme time poem (see page 89) if desired.

Now who is this a-tapping?

Ready, steady, go

- ✪ **Aim:** To affirm that bold asking is an aspect of prayer
- ✪ **Truth:** God is listening and wants us to pray boldly for our friends
- ✪ **Themes:** Caring, asking, friendship and emotions

Biblical basis: Prayer

Then Jesus went on to say: Suppose one of you goes to a friend in the middle of the night and says, 'Let me borrow three loaves of bread. A friend of mine has dropped in, and I don't have a thing for him to eat.' And suppose your friend answers, 'Don't bother me! The door is bolted, and my children and I are in bed. I cannot get up to give you something.'

He may not get up and give you the bread, just because you are his friend. But he will get up and give you as much as you need, simply because you are not ashamed to keep on asking.

So I tell you to ask and you will receive, search and you will find, knock and the door will be opened for you. Everyone who asks will receive, everyone who searches will find, and the door will be opened for everyone who knocks.'

LUKE 11:5–10

In a circle

Name tag teddy

> **Time guide: 5 minutes**
>
> **You will need:** A teddy name tag for each child (see page 64 for photocopiable template), coloured pens, pencils or crayons, a hole punch, sticky tape, scissors and a length of ribbon

Help the children to cut out and colour their tags and write their names on the front. Place sticky tape toward the top, where you will punch a hole. Loop ribbon through the hole and tie the ends.

Pat-a-pet

Sleepy Ted

> **Time guide: 5 minutes**
>
> **You will need:** A teddy bear

Cradle Sleepy Ted in your arms as if he is sleeping. Whisper to the children that Sleepy Ted is a visitor for the day.

Welcomes and waves

Good morning, Sleepy Ted

 Time guide: 5 minutes

You will need: Sleepy Ted pat-a-pet, the following rhyme and a helper to lead

All together: *Good morning, Sleepy Ted. Good morning to you!*
Child holding Sleepy Ted: *My name is [child's name]. How do you do?*

Explain that you need help waking Sleepy Ted. You are going to pass Sleepy Ted around the circle. Everyone will repeat the rhyme together. The child holding Sleepy Ted may kiss, hug or tickle him to help wake him up and will put his or her own name into the rhyme before passing Sleepy Ted to the next child.

Story sack

Now who is this a-tapping?

 Time guide: 5 minutes

You will need: Tired Tim (beanie doll dressed in pyjamas), Pesky Pete (beanie doll dressed in pyjamas and dressing-gown), a doll's blanket, pillow and little teddy, a bed made from a shoebox, an alarm clock with the hands set at midnight, a bread bin with a loaf of bread in it, a shoebox containing a pair of rhythm sticks or wooden spoons for each child (optional)

You will wear: Pyjamas

Dress in pyjamas. Hold the story sack in your lap until everyone in the circle is seated and settled. Instruct the children that they are not to move from where they are sitting unless told to do so. Quietly set up the scene as follows:

Remove the shoebox and place it in front of you. Remove the pillow and put it in the shoebox. Remove Tired Tim and cradle him in your arms. Whisper 'Shhhh' to the children and pretend Tired Tim is snoring as you gently place him in the shoebox. Remove the blanket and cover Tired Tim. Remove the little teddy and tuck it

in next to Tired Tim. Remove the alarm clock and the bread bin and sit them next to the shoebox. Keep Pesky Pete hidden, but easily accessible, in the story sack behind your back.

Optional: Remove the shoebox containing the rhythm sticks or wooden spoons. Explain in a whisper that Sleepy Ted spilled some pretend honey on the sticks (or spoons) when he was eating his breakfast and that they are very sticky. Tell the children that a helper will come to them where they are in the circle and give them a pair of sticks or spoons. They are to hold these as if they are stuck together with honey until you tell them what to do. Demonstrate. To minimize the shuffle, remind the children that Tired Tim is asleep in his bed. Once the children have their sticks or spoons, tell them to pretend to lick the honey off and hold one in each hand. They are not to tap them together until you ask them to do so.

Tell the children that you will need their help in the story. They are to knock on the floor or, if using sticks or spoons, tap them together once on each 'T' sound they hear in the words 'tap and 'tappit', then keep their sticks or spoons still again. Have a quiet group practice of the first verse.

Tell the following rhyme time parable, following the directions in roman (upright) type.

Rhyme time

Now who is this a-tapping?

 Time guide: 10 minutes

(Make snoring sounds)
Now who is this a-tapping
On Tired Tim's door?
(Look around the circle quizzically)
Tap tappit! Tap tappit!
(Encourage the children to tap their fists, sticks or spoons on the 'T' sounds)
At midnight or more?
(Pick up the clock, point to midnight and put it down again)

Tired Tim's peeking out,
(Get Tired Tim up out of his bed)
Pesky Pete's peeking in.
(Bring Pesky Pete from behind your back to face Tired Tim)
'Have you got any bread?'
(Move Pesky Pete as if he is speaking)
He says with a grin.

'Pete, you're a pest,
Please come back when it is day!'
(Move Tired Tim as if speaking; then wander him back to bed, where he crawls under the covers, kisses his teddy and begins to snore)
I wonder, do you wonder,
(Look at Pesky Pete)
Will Pete go away?
(Put Pesky Pete behind your back again)

(Make snoring sounds)
Now who is this a-tapping
On Tired Tim's door?
(Look around quizzically)
Tap tappit! Tap tappit!
(Encourage the children to tap their fists, sticks or spoons on the 'T' sounds)
Interrupting a snore!

Tired Tim's peeking out,
(Get Tired Tim up out of his bed with a sigh)
Pesky Pete's peeking in.
(Bring Pesky Pete from behind your back to face Tired Tim)
'The bread is for a friend,'
(Move Pesky Pete as if he is speaking)
He says. 'Please let me in'.

'Please, Pesky Pete,
Come back when it is day!'
(Move Tired Tim as if speaking; then wander him back to bed, where he crawls under the covers, kisses his teddy and begins to snore)
I wonder, do you wonder,
(Look at Pesky Pete)
Will Pete go away?
(Put Pesky Pete behind your back again)

(Make snoring sounds)
Now who is this a-tapping
On Tired Tim's door?
(Look around quizzically)
Tap tappit! Tap tappit!
(Encourage the children to tap their fists, sticks or spoons on the 'T' sounds)
We've heard it before!

Tired Tim's peeking out,
(Get Tired Tim up out of his bed with a sigh)
Pesky Pete's peeking in,
(Bring Pesky Pete from behind your back to face Tired Tim)
'All right,' says Tim,
(Move Tired Tim as if speaking)
There's some bread in my bin!'

(Open the bread bin to reveal the bread. Tired Tim gives Pesky Pete a hug and takes the bread away behind your back. Tired Tim wanders back to bed, crawls under the covers, kisses his teddy and starts snoring)

I wonder, do you wonder,
(Look around quizzically)
Does God have a clock?
(Pick up clock, shake head 'no', put clock behind your back)
When we pray, night or day
(Fold hands)
God is there when we knock.
(Knock twice on the floor)

When you are finished, whisper to the children that they are to stay seated until their names are called. When they hear their names, they are to tiptoe to the box, quietly put their sticks back in it and tiptoe back to their place in the circle. When they have finished, quietly remove the scene, talking about each item as you return it to the story sack.

Chat about
Chat about what the children liked best about this story. Use some of the following wondering questions:

✪ I wonder who you would most like to be in the story?
✪ I wonder what it feels like to get woken up when you are trying to sleep?
✪ I wonder if God ever sleeps?
✪ I wonder why Pesky Pete wouldn't wait until morning?
✪ I wonder who came to visit Pesky Pete late at night?
✪ I wonder how we can pray for our friends?

Up and about with tickle trunk

 Time guide: 10 minutes

You will need: Two sets of oversized pyjamas, two pairs of slippers, two dressing-gowns, two nightcaps, two blankets, two teddies, an alarm clock, a blanket and pillow and some pretend bread

Either encourage the children to play freely with the parable in their own way or choose a cast of children to act out the rhyme time parable.

'We can' can

We can sing about bedtime

(Tune: Here we go round the mulberry bush)

 Time guide: 5 minutes

You will need: The 'We can' can, containing the words and actions below.

This is the way we take a bath, take a bath, take a bath.
This is the way we take a bath, take a bath at bedtime.
(Pretend to wash)

This is the way we put on our nightclothes…
put on our nightclothes at bedtime.
(Pretend to dress)

This is the way we brush our teeth…
brush our teeth at bedtime.
(Pretend to brush your teeth)

This is the way we wash our face…
wash our face at bedtime.
(Pretend to wash your face)

This is the way we read a book…
read a book at bedtime.
(Pretend to read a book)

This is the way we say our prayers…
say our prayers at bedtime.
(Pretend to pray)

This is the way we cuddle our teds…
cuddle our teds at bedtime.
(Pretend to cuddle your teddy)

This is the way we give a kiss…
give a kiss at bedtime.
(Pretend to kiss)

This is the way we go to sleep…
go to sleep at bedtime.
(Pretend to go to sleep)

Choose a child to remove the instructions from the 'We can' can. Say, 'We can sing about bedtime!' Sing the song together. Remember to involve your Sleepy Ted pat-a-pet.

Chat about

Chat about what the children like best about bedtime.

Food fun

Sleepy Ted sandwiches

 Time guide: 10 minutes

You will need: Teddy bear biscuit cutters, the loaf of bread used in the story, butter, honey, child-safe knives for spreading and lots of baby wipes or paper towels for sticky fingers.

Give each child a slice of bread, a teddy biscuit cutter and a knife. Allow the children to cut their own teddies. Help them to spread butter and honey on their teddies. Eat up and clean up.

Chat about

Chat about what Pesky Pete wanted from Tired Tim. What good things does God give us to share with our friends?

Prayer pocket

Share-a-prayer cards

 Time guide: 5 minutes

You will need: A prayer pocket decorated with a picture of a teddy, an envelope and a sheet of share-a-prayer cards for each child (see templates on page 72), an extra set of prayer cards for the prayer pocket, colouring pens, pencils, crayons, gummy shapes, glitter glue, scissors

Encourage the children to cut out and decorate their share-a-prayer cards and to decorate their envelopes. When they have finished, ask one of the children to take the contents from the prayer pocket. Read the prayer cards together and discuss the pictures on them. Explore some of the 'Chat about' questions below.

Chat about

Chat about how God helps us to be brave. How does God keep us company? Ask the children to tell you about a time when they felt unwell, were worried, or had a problem that they needed help with. What kinds of things does God give us?

Finish by using the prayer cards as flash cards for group prayer. Hold each card up in turn and encourage the children to fill in the blanks:

Dear God, please help… to feel better.
Dear God, please help… to be brave.
Dear God, please be close to…
Dear God, please give… what they need.
Dear God, please help… not to worry.
Dear God, please help… to know what to do.

Home and away link

Send the share-a-prayer cards home with each child. 'Home and away' provides a further linked activity.

Busy box

'Thinking of you' teddies

 Time guide: 10 minutes

You will need: 'Thinking of you' teddy template copied on to coloured card (see photocopiable sheet on page 66), colouring pens, pencils, crayons, gummy shapes, glitter glue, scissors

Invite the children to cut out and decorate their 'Thinking of you' teddies. Set them aside to dry. Encourage the children to talk to their parents or carers about who needs prayer and who they might give the finished card to.

Go game

Pyjama relay

 Time guide: 5 minutes

You will need: Three sets of oversized nightshirts, sleeping caps, slippers, pillows, blankets and teddies

Form the children into a large circle and ask them to sit down. Place each set of props in a different spot in the middle of the circle. Choose three volunteers from among the children and show them which prop pile each volunteer is to use.

When the leader says 'Go', the children run to their respective props, put on a nightshirt, sleeping cap and slippers, tuck under the blanket with the teddy and place their head on the pillow. The quickest one wins. Help the children to take off the props and play again with three other children.

Music makers

Hickory dickory dock

 Time guide: 5 minutes

You will need: A clock, a jingle bell or triangle for every child and the following words.

Hickory dickory dock,
The mouse ran up the clock.
The clock struck… [any number from one to twelve]
The mouse ran down,
Hickory dickory dock.

Explain to the children that you are going to sing the song 'Hickory dickory dock' together. Instruct them to hold their instruments completely still. When the clock strikes in the song, you will say and point to the number one on the clock in your hand. They are to shake their bell or strike their triangle once. Have a practice. Explain that you will sing the song again but this time the clock will strike a different number. You will say and point to the number on the clock in your hand. The children are to shake their bell or strike their triangle the same number of times. Repeat this activity several times before collecting the instruments. You could use Sleepy Ted to point to the clock.

Chat about

Chat about what is the children's favourite time of day.

Memory time

 Time guide: 5 minutes

You will need: The Bible verse 'Jesus said, "Ask and you will receive"' (Luke 11:9a)

Teach the children the following actions. Explain that remembering what is said in the Bible can really help us, and that they are going to try to remember something Jesus said, using both words and actions.

Jesus said, 'Ask': Touch lips with right index finger.
'And you will receive': Open both hands out in front of you, palms up, and move them back toward your body until your palms touch your heart.

Practise the actions to the verse yourself in advance of the session.

Chat about

Chat about how the children feel when they knock on a friend's door. How do they feel when they ask for something and get what they asked for?

Home and away

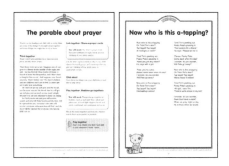

Give each child a copy of Home and Away Sheet 7 (see page 80) and a copy of the 'Now who is this a-tapping?' rhyme time poem (see page 90) if desired.

Good shepherd had a little lamb

Ready, steady, go

- ✪ **Aim:** To affirm God's love and care for each child
- ✪ **Truth:** God loves us and wants to help us when we are lonely and afraid
- ✪ **Themes:** Emotions, lost and found, and work

Biblical basis: One sheep

Then Jesus told them this story: If any of you has a hundred sheep, and one of them gets lost, what will you do? Won't you leave the ninety-nine in the field and go and look for the lost sheep until you find it? And when you find it, you will be so glad that you will put it on your shoulder and carry it home. Then you will call in your friends and neighbours and say, 'Let's celebrate! I've found my lost sheep.'

Jesus said, 'In the same way there is more happiness in heaven because of one sinner who turns to God than over ninety-nine good people who don't need to.'

LUKE 15:3–7

In a circle

Name tag lamb

 Time guide: 5 minutes

You will need: A lamb name tag for each child (see page 64 for photocopiable template), coloured pens, pencils or crayons, a hole punch, sticky tape, scissors and a length of ribbon

Help the children to cut out and colour their tags and write their names on the front. Place sticky tape toward the top, where you will punch a hole. Loop ribbon through the hole and tie the ends.

Pat-a-pet

Little Lamb

 Time guide: **5 minutes**

You will need: A lamb soft toy or puppet

Introduce Little Lamb to the group as a visitor for the day. Pass Little Lamb around the circle so that everyone can give Little Lamb a welcome hug.

Welcomes and waves

One little lamb goes out to play

 Time guide: 5 minutes

You will need: Little Lamb pat-a-pet, the following rhyme and a helper to lead

Every time:
Little lamb [name a child] goes out to play,
Leaps up high and baas 'hooray!'

Last time:
And when the stars are in the sky
The lambs bounce home and wave goodbye.

Hold Little Lamb and explain that everyone is going to pretend to be a lamb. Instruct the children to stay seated until their names are called. When their name is heard, they are to stand up and leap like a lamb. When all the lambs are up and leaping, the helper will lead in waving goodbye and everyone will sit down again.

Have a quick group practice of leaping so that the children will feel comfortable when their turn comes. When you have completed the welcome once through, you may want to do it again. To make it harder, toss Little Lamb to the child whose name is called and encourage that child to say another child's name and pass Little Lamb on.

Story sack

Good Shepherd had a little lamb

 Time guide: 5 minutes

You will need: A beanie doll dressed as a shepherd, some small confetti flowers, two identical lambs, one hidden behind a posy of silk flowers, a flock of several other toy sheep, a blanket for the shepherd, a tree shape with a little bird hidden under a leaf in its branches, some little stones and a bigger rock with a picture of a frog taped to the bottom, a blue scarf, a green cloth, a moon made from tin foil and some confetti stars

You will wear: Shepherd clothes, and carry a shepherd's crook

Dress like a shepherd. Hold the story sack in your lap until everyone in the circle is seated and settled. Instruct the children that they are not to move from where they are sitting unless told to do so. Quietly set up the scene.

Remove the green cloth from the story sack and lay it out like a field on the floor in front of you. It does not have to be flat. Remove the blue scarf and lay it like a river on the green cloth. Remove the rocks and place them in the scene (do not reveal the hidden frog). Remove the tree and place it in the scene (do not reveal the hidden bird). Remove the small flowers and sprinkle them in the scene. Remove the posy of silk flowers and place it in the scene (do not reveal the lamb). Remove several sheep and place them in a flock in the scene.

Tell the following rhyme time parable, following the directions in roman (upright) type.

Rhyme time

Good Shepherd had a little lamb

 Time guide: 10 minutes

Good Shepherd had a little lamb
(Remove, show and place the shepherd in the scene)
Whose fleece was white as snow,
(Remove, show and place the lamb with the flock in the scene)
And everywhere Good Shepherd went
(Move the shepherd along the stream in the scene)
The lamb was sure to go.
(Move the lamb to follow the shepherd)

(Remove the blanket and lay the shepherd under it as if sleeping. Remove the lamb without the children noticing too much and tuck it out of sight)

Then one day Good Shepherd woke.
(Remove the shepherd from the blanket and stand him up)
His lamb he could not see.
I wonder, do you wonder,
Where Little Lamb could be?

Lamb, are you behind the tree?
(Move the shepherd to the tree. Lift the leaf to reveal the bird)
Are you beside the stone?
(Move the shepherd to the large stone. Lift the stone to reveal the frog)
Oh, Little Lamb, where are you?
You're lost and all alone!

Soon it will be night-time.
(Show the moon and sprinkle confetti stars)
Shhh, there in the grass!
(Move the shepherd to the posy of flowers)
Good Shepherd's found his little lamb,
(Reveal the lost sheep)
Happiness at last!
(The shepherd hugs and kisses the lamb)

'I've found my lamb!' Good Shepherd says,
(Take the shepherd and sheep in your hand and
motion round the circle making eye contact with
the children)
Laughing with a leap!
'Let's have a party right away
And invite the other sheep!'
(Put the lamb and the shepherd among the other
sheep in the scene)

I wonder, do you wonder,
Who might Good Shepherd be?
Jesus is the shepherd
Who cares for you and me.
(Gesture 'you and me' with an open palm around
the circle)

Chat about

Chat about what the children liked best about this story.
Use some of the following wondering questions:

 I wonder who you would most like to be in the story?
 I wonder if you have ever been lost?
 I wonder why Little Lamb wandered away?
 I wonder how Little Lamb felt when Good Shepherd found him?
 I wonder how we are like Little Lamb?
 I wonder how Jesus is like Good Shepherd?

When you are finished, quietly remove the scene, talking
about each item as you return it to the story sack.

Up and about with tickle trunk

Time guide: 10 minutes

You will need: A large green sheet or other
piece of fabric (field); a fold-up Christmas tree
or bits of real tree branches (tree); a long piece
of blue fabric or several blue scarves tied
together (river); some brown paper bags
stuffed with newspaper (rocks); dungarees or
overalls, wellies, walking stick, hat (shepherd);

toy frogs, a toy bird, several silk or paper flowers,
a blanket or sleeping bag, several sheep costumes
or masks, or several soft toy sheep, a large tin foil
moon, several kinds and types of stars

Either encourage the children to play freely with the
parable in their own way or choose a cast of children to
act out the rhyme time parable.

'We can' can

We can sing 'Good Shepherd went over the mountain'

(Tune: The bear went over the mountain)

 Time guide: **5 minutes**

You will need: The 'We can' can, containing a
slip of paper that says, 'We can sing "Good
Shepherd went over the mountain" and the
following words.

Good Shepherd went over the mountain (x 3)
To see what he could see.
And what do you think he saw? (x 2)
The other side of the mountain (x 3)
Was all that he could see.

So what do you think he did? (x 2)
He went back over the mountain (x 3)
To see what he could see.
And what do you think he saw? (x 2)
The other side of the mountain (x 3)
Was all that he could see.

Good Shepherd hopped over the mountain…
Good Shepherd skipped up the mountain…
Good Shepherd ran round the mountain…
Good Shepherd marched over the mountain…
Good Shepherd tiptoed up the mountain…
Good Shepherd climbed up the mountain…
Good Shepherd stamped up the mountain…

Last time:
Good Shepherd went over the mountain (x 3)
To see what he could see.
And what do you think he saw? (x 2)
Little Lamb on the mountain: (x 3)
They had a great party!

Choose a child to remove the instructions from the 'We can' can. Sing the song and do the actions as a group.

Chat about
Chat about how it feels to look for something lost.

Food fun

Silly sheep

 Time guide: 10 minutes

You will need: Party favours, balloons, poppers and hats, large white marshmallows, shop-bought chocolate sauce, Rice Krispies, a paper plate and fork for each child, lots of baby wipes or paper towels for sticky fingers

Put some chocolate sauce in several bowls. Give each child a paper plate, a fork and a marshmallow. Help each child to place a marshmallow on his or her fork, dunk it completely in the chocolate sauce and roll it in Rice Krispies. Eat up and clean up.

Chat about
Chat about what kind of party we would have for someone we love.

Prayer pocket

Body bits collage

 Time guide: 5 minutes

You will need: A prayer pocket decorated with pictures of people, a large piece of card, sticky tape and the following items cut from various magazine photos: one head, two ears, two eyes, one nose, one mouth, two arms, two hands, one body, two legs and two feet

Put the body bits into the prayer pocket before the session. When it's time, have several children take out one body bit at a time and, as a group, sticky tape the collage person together on the card.

Chat about
Chat about the ways in which people are the same as each other. In what ways are people different from each other? Why are we each so special to God? How are we special to each other? Finish with the following prayer.

Thank you, God, I can pray when I'm thinking
(Point to head)
Thank you, God, I can pray when I'm blinking
(Blink)
Thank you, God, I can pray when I'm walking
(Walk on the spot)
Thank you, God, I can pray when I'm talking
(Mime talking)
Thank you, God, I can pray with my hands
(Fold hands)
Thank you, God, I can pray when I stand (Stand tall)
Thank you, God, I can pray as I hear (Cup ear)
Thank you, God, I can pray when I cheer
(Shout hooray)
Thank you, God, for as you see
(Hold hands out with palms up)
I can pray to you with the whole of me!
(Twirl around)

Busy box

Matching animals

 Time guide: 10 minutes

You will need: Scissors, crayons, a sheet of matching animal mums and babies for each child, copied on to card (see photocopiable sheet on page 67)

Help the children colour and cut out the pictures. Demonstrate how they may be used in a matching game by mixing one set of the pictures up and placing each one face up on a table or the floor. Find the matching mother and baby. To make this more difficult, mix a set of the pictures up and place them face down. Two pictures are then turned over to see if they match. If not, they are turned face down again. If they do match, they are withdrawn from the playing area and set aside. The players must try to remember where the matching pictures are. Two players can play with one set of cards.

Chat about
Chat about the people who love and care for us. How can we show that we care about someone?

Home and away link
Send a set of matching animal cards home with each child. 'Home and away' provides a further linked activity.

Go game

Follow the shepherd

 Time guide: 5 minutes

You will need: A leader to be the shepherd, Little Lamb pat-a-pet

Choose a shepherd from among the helpers. Tell the children that they are sheep and must follow the shepherd and Little Lamb and do what they do: for example, skip, jump, walk sideways, fairy step, giant step, run, crawl, bounce along on their bottoms and so on. After a while, choose a child to be the shepherd, give the child Little Lamb to hold, and play again.

Chat about

Chat about how we can follow Jesus.

Music makers

Animal bumps

 Time guide: 5 minutes

You will need: A soft toy farm animal for each child, music, a carpet square for each child

Let each child choose a soft toy. Set the carpet squares in a circle. Ensure that there is enough room to walk around the outside safely. When the music is playing, the children must circle around the outside of the carpet squares. When the music stops, the children must quickly sit down on the nearest square and make the sound of their animal. Start the music and play again.

Chat about

Chat about the kind of pets the children have. How do they care for their pets?

Memory time

 Time guide: 5 minutes

You will need: The Bible verse 'Jesus is the good shepherd' (John 10:14, paraphrased)

Teach the children the following actions. Explain that remembering what is said in the Bible can really help us, and that they are going to try to remember something the Bible says, using both words and actions.

> **Jesus:** Touch middle finger of the right hand to the palm of the left and vice versa.
>
> **Is the good shepherd:** Pretend to hold and pet a lamb.

Practise the actions to the verse yourself in advance of the session.

Chat about

Chat about how we know that someone loves us. How does Jesus show us that he loves us?

Home and away

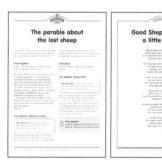

Give each child a copy of Home and Away Sheet 8 (see page 81) and a copy of the 'Good Shepherd had a little lamb' rhyme time poem (see page 91) if desired.

53

Silly Billy

- ✪ **Aim:** To affirm that God is a loving parent
- ✪ **Truth:** God forgives us when we ask him to
- ✪ **Themes:** Emotions, family, animals, lost and found, and city life

Biblical basis: The lost son

Once a man had two sons. The younger son said to his father, 'Give me my share of the property.' So the father divided his property between his two sons.

Not long after that, the younger son packed up everything he owned and left for a foreign country, where he wasted all his money in wild living. He had spent everything, when a bad famine spread through that whole land. Soon he had nothing to eat.

He went to work for a man in that country, and the man sent him out to take care of his pigs. He would have been glad to eat what the pigs were eating, but no one gave him a thing.

Finally, he came to his senses and said, 'My father's workers have plenty to eat, and here I am, starving to death! I will go to my father and say to him, "Father, I have sinned against God in heaven and against you. I am no longer good enough to be called your son. Treat me like one of your workers."'

The younger son got up and started back to his father. But when he was still a long way off, his father saw him and felt sorry for him. He ran to his son and hugged and kissed him.

The son said, 'Father, I have sinned against God in heaven and against you. I am no longer good enough to be called your son.'

But his father said to the servants, 'Hurry and bring the best clothes and put them on him. Give him a ring for his finger and sandals for his feet. Get the best calf and prepare it, so we can eat and celebrate. This son of mine was dead, but has now come back to life. He was lost and has now been found.' And they began to celebrate.

LUKE 15:11–24

In a circle

Name tag pig

> Time guide: 5 minutes
>
> **You will need:** A pig name tag for each child (see page 64 for photocopiable template), coloured pens, pencils or crayons, a hole punch, sticky tape, scissors and a length of ribbon

Help the children to cut out and colour their tags and write their names on the front. Place sticky tape toward the top, where you will punch a hole. Loop ribbon through the hole and tie the ends.

Pat-a-pet

Rig-a-jig Pig

 Time guide: 5 minutes

You will need: A pig soft toy or puppet

Introduce Rig-a-jig Pig to the group as a visitor for the day. Get the children to grunt a piggy 'hello'.

Welcomes and waves

Rig-a-jig Pig

 Time guide: 5 minutes

You will need: Rig-a-jig Pig soft toy and a helper to lead the following chant

[Child's name, repeated twice] likes to [activity]
But Rig-a-jig Pig likes to dance a jig.
(All stand up and do a little jig and sit down again)

Explain that Rig-a-jig Pig likes to dance a jig. Ask the children what they like to do, then explain that when you say someone's name, that person is to tell everyone something that they like to do. For example, 'Sam, Sam likes to swim.' Whenever you say, 'Rig-a-jig Pig likes to dance a jig', everyone is to stand up, do a small dance and sit down again. Remember to involve Rig-a-jig Pig.

Suggested activities might include ride on the swing, eat chocolate, play ball, take a nap, run and jump, hop, skip, play with toys, swim and so on.

Story sack

Silly Billy

 Time guide: 5 minutes

You will need: A simple homemade play mat with a farm on one end, a road leading to the city on the other end and a pig farm in the middle; farm animals and machinery to accessorize play mat; things you might find in a city to accessorize play mat; some toy pigs for the pig farm; a toy

person, car and money (Silly Billy); a father figure doll (father); other figure dolls (friends); a set of new clothes, a ring, party snacks for everyone

You will wear: Old ragged clothes

Dress in ragged clothes. Hold the story sack in your lap until everyone in the circle is seated and settled. Instruct the children that they are not to move from where they are sitting unless told to do so. Quietly set up the scene.

Remove the play mat and place it on the floor in front of you. Remove the farm animals and machinery and place them on the play mat farm. Remove the city things and place them on the play mat city. Remove the pigs and place them on the pig farm.

Tell the following rhyme time parable, following the directions in roman (upright) type.

Rhyme time

Silly Billy

 Time guide: 10 minutes

(Remove Silly Billy from the story sack)
Oh where have you been,
Billy boy, Billy boy?
Oh where have you been,
Silly Billy?

I have run away from home,
To the city I have gone,
(Remove the car, put Silly Billy in it and drive it from the farm to the city)
And I have left my father.
(Remove father and place him at the farm as if looking for the son)

What did you do,
Billy boy, Billy boy?
What did you do,
Silly Billy?

I threw a party, and had some fun,
(Remove friends and put them in the city; one friend steals car and drives away)
Forgot my father back at home.
But now my money is all gone.
(Remove money and throw it in the air as if it has all been spent)

Where do you live,
Billy boy, Billy boy?
Where do you live,
Silly Billy?

I'm very hungry and alone,
I eat with pigs, oh how I moan.
(Walk Silly Billy to pig farm and put him among the pigs)
I miss my father and my home.

I wonder, do you wonder,
Billy boy, Billy boy?
Will he want you back again,
Silly Billy?

I know my father loves me so.
To God in heaven I will go
And say, 'Forgive me, father.'
(Begin to walk Billy back home)

Is he waiting by the gate,
Billy boy, Billy boy?
Is he waiting by the gate,
Silly Billy?

He is running, arms out wide,
Hugs and kisses, joy inside.
'Safe at last!' my father cried.
(Billy and his father run to one another and embrace)

Does he want you to come in,
Billy boy, Billy boy?
Does he want you to come in,
Silly Billy?

There's a party just for me,
New clothes, a ring and tea.
(Remove clothes, ring and party snacks)
I am back home with my father!

I wonder, do you wonder,
Billy boy, Billy boy?
Does God forgive every
Silly Billy?
(Point with open hand round the circle and to self)

Yes, God forgives us every one,
No matter what we've said or done.
God is a kind and loving Father.
(Give everyone a party snack)

Chat about

Chat about what the children liked best about this story. Use some of the following wondering questions:

 I wonder what you would change about this story?
 I wonder why Billy ran away from such a kind father?
 I wonder what Billy spent his money on?
 I wonder why Billy's father kept waiting for him?
 I wonder if Billy liked his party and presents?
 I wonder if you have ever been a Silly Billy?
 I wonder how it feels to be forgiven?

When you are finished, quietly remove the scene, talking about each item as you return it to the story sack.

Up and about with tickle trunk

🕐 Time guide: 10 minutes

You will need: A set of oversized ragged clothes (Billy), a backpack, moneybag and toy money, a ride-on car, a set of oversized farming clothes (father), waistcoats and hats (friends), toy shop and register, toy pigs or pig masks, a set of oversized fancy party clothes, ring and shoes (Billy), party hats, streamers and pretend food

Either encourage the children to play freely with the parable in their own way or choose a cast of children to act out the rhyme time parable.

'We can' can

We can play 'Who's missing?'

🕐 Time guide: 5 minutes

You will need: The 'We can' can containing a slip of paper that says, 'We can play "Who's missing?"' and the following instructions.

The children sit in a circle and one child is sent away where he cannot see or hear what is happening. Another child is chosen to hide out of sight. The first child returns and tries to guess who is missing. If he cannot remember, the other children can offer clues, such as something the child is wearing or the first letter of their name.

Chat about

Chat about how it feels when we can't be with someone we love.

Food fun

Prodigal pudding

 Time guide: 10 minutes

You will need: One empty ice cream cone and plastic spoon per child, pre-made chocolate mousse or angel delight, mini pink marshmallows, a spoon, baby wipes

Give each child a plastic spoon and cone. Help them to fill their cones with mud (chocolate mousse or angel delight), and sprinkle on some pigs (mini pink marshmallows). Eat up and clean up.

Chat about
Chat about what it would be like to live with pigs. How might it feel to be hungry and alone? What are the children's favourite foods?

Prayer pocket

I spy binoculars

 Time guide: 5 minutes

You will need: A prayer pocket decorated like a pair of binoculars, two card tubes per child, colours, stickers and sticky tape

Decorate the tubes and tape them together. Play a game of 'I spy with my little eye…' using things that the children might see if they were waiting for someone to come home, such as a bus passing by, children walking by, a postman, cars, birds, neighbours, trees, flowers, the moon or sun and so on.

Finish with the following prayer.

I thank you, God, for what I see,
Thank you, God, for watching me! Amen

Home and away link
Send the binoculars home with each child. 'Home and away' provides a further linked activity.

Chat about
Chat about who the children would like to visit them. Is there someone they can't wait to see, or someone they love to hug?

Busy box

Felt faces

 Time guide: 10 minutes

You will need: Cardboard, sandpaper, scissors, several colours of felt, PVA glue, pen or marker, containers

Cut several oval shapes out of sandpaper and glue them on to cardboard to make faces. Cut facial features, such as eyes, noses, eyebrows, mouths, eyeglasses, ears, moustaches and hair out of felt. Make faces with different expressions, such as sad, glad, surprised, frightened or cross.

Chat about
Chat about a time when the children were sad. Can they tell about a time they were glad or surprised? What makes them angry? What gives them a fright?

Go game

Hanky tug

 Time guide: 5 minutes

You will need: A hula hoop and three hankies for each group of three children

Three equally spaced children hold tightly to each hoop. Place a hanky just beyond reach behind each child. When you say 'Go', the children must pull as hard as they can on the hoop with one hand while trying to reach their hanky with the other.

Music makers

Pass the tissues

 Time guide: 5 minutes

You will need: A box of tissues

Sit the children in a circle and give one child the tissue box. Explain that the box will be passed from one child to the next while the music is playing. When the music stops, the child holding the box must pull a tissue out of it and pretend to blow his or her nose.

Chat about

Chat about how we can help people who are sad.

Memory time

 Time guide: 5 minutes

You will need: The Bible verse 'God's love is for ever' (1 Chronicles 16:34, paraphrased)

Teach the children the following actions. Explain that remembering what is said in the Bible can really help us, and that they are going to try to remember something the Bible says, using both words and actions.

God's:	Point up for God.
Love:	Hug yourself.
Is for ever:	Use index fingers to make spiralling motion from your heart outward in both directions from the body.

Practise the actions to the verse yourself in advance of the session.

Chat about

Chat about how long 'for ever' is.

Home and away

Give each child a copy of Home and Away Sheet 9 (see page 82) and a copy of the 'Silly Billy' rhyme time poem (see page 92) if desired.

We have a little garden

- **Aim:** To affirm that great things grow from small seeds
- **Truth:** God's kingdom flourishes from small beginnings
- **Themes:** Growing, animals, friendship, seasons and work

Biblical basis: A mustard seed

Jesus said, 'What is God's kingdom like? What can I compare it with? It is like what happens when someone plants a mustard seed in a garden. The seed grows as big as a tree, and birds nest in its branches.'

LUKE 13:18–19

In a circle

Name tag caterpillar

 Time guide: **5 minutes**

You will need: A caterpillar name tag for each child (see page 64 for photocopiable template), coloured pens, pencils or crayons, a hole punch, sticky tape, scissors and a length of ribbon

Help the children to cut out and colour their tags and write their names on the front. Place sticky tape toward the top, where you will punch a hole. Loop ribbon through the hole and tie the ends.

Pat-a-pet

Creep-along Caterpillar

 Time guide: **5 minutes**

You will need: A caterpillar soft toy or puppet

Introduce Creep-along Caterpillar to the group with the following rhyme.

Who's that creeping very slowly up the garden wall?
(Crawl the caterpillar up your arm)
'Me,' says Creep-along, 'I'm learning to crawl!'

Welcomes and waves

There's a little caterpillar

 Time guide: **5 minutes**

You will need: Creep-along Caterpillar, a helper to lead and the following rhyme

There's a little caterpillar in that tree! (Point)
How many leaf holes can we see? (Pretend to look)
Come along, [name a child], tiptoe with me. (Named child tiptoes behind the leader)
Let's count the leaf holes: one, two, three. (Stop and count on fingers)

Explain that caterpillars eat leaves, so we are looking to see if Creep-along has had his breakfast yet! When you say someone's name, that child is to stand up and tiptoe behind you. Pass Creep-along Caterpillar to the child to hold. Repeat the chant, passing Creep-along to each new child as he or she is named, until everyone is following the leader. During the last time, lead the children to sit back down in the circle and collect Creep-along from the child at the end of the line.

Story sack

We have a little garden

 Time guide: 5 minutes

You will need: A floppy garden hat, a watering can filled with blue confetti, tinsel or shredded paper for water, gardening gloves, a basket full of garden-themed soft toys, large silk flowers, a paper nest and some silk birds

You will wear: Gardening clothes (jacket, gloves, boots and so on)

Dress like a gardener. Hold the story sack in your lap until everyone in the circle is seated and settled. Instruct the children that they are not to move from where they are sitting unless told to do so. Quietly set up the scene.

Remove the floppy hat and garden gloves and put them on. Remove the watering can and set it aside. Remove the basket of garden-themed puppets, soft toys and silk flowers. Bring the basket around the circle and let the children choose something from it. Save the nest of birds for one of the leaders. Everyone is to crouch down and be seeds until you tap them on the shoulder and help them to grow.

Tell the following rhyme time parable, following the directions in roman (upright) type.

Rhyme time

We have a little garden

 Time guide: 10 minutes

We have a little garden,
A garden all our own,
(Stand up in the middle of the 'garden' and motion round the circle)
And every day we water there
The seed that we have sown.
(Walk around the circle with the watering can and sprinkle each 'seed' with a fistful of 'water')

And every day, no matter what,
We watch and wait and pray.
(Pretend to watch and pray)
I wonder, do you wonder,
Will our seed grow today?
(Finger on chin)

See, our seed is growing,
(Go around the circle and touch each 'seed' on the head to help them grow)
Our seed that was so small
Has grown into a nesting tree,
Big and strong and tall.
(Touch the leader with the birds and help them grow into a tall and branching tree with the nest high in one hand)

We are in God's garden,
He tends us with such care.
(Motion around the circle and point up towards heaven)
He warms us with his love
(Give yourself a cuddle)
And waters us with prayer.
(Fold hands in prayer)

I wonder, do you wonder,
What you and I will be?
(Motion around the circle, pointing to the children and then to yourself)
Every day, no matter what,
We'll wait and pray and see!
(Motion to everyone to sit down again)

Chat about

Chat about what the children liked best about this story. Use some of the following wondering questions:

- I wonder what it is like to wait for a seed to grow?
- I wonder what it is like to be as big and strong as a tree?
- I wonder if the nesting birds are glad to find rest and shade?
- I wonder if the person who planted the seed was amazed by what it became?
- I wonder how Jesus can help us grow big and strong?
- I wonder where we can find rest and shade?

When you are finished, quietly remove the scene, talking about each item as you return it to the story sack.

Up and about with tickle trunk

> **Time guide: 10 minutes**
>
> **You will need:** Floppy hats, garden-themed soft toys, silk flowers, garden gloves, watering cans, plastic gardening tools, silk leaves and birds

Either encourage the children to play freely with the parable in their own way or choose a cast of children to act out the rhyme time parable.

'We can' can

We can do the caterpillar crawl

> **Time guide: 5 minutes**
>
> **You will need:** A slip of paper that says, 'We can do the caterpillar crawl' and the following words

A caterpillar crawled up an old oak tree.
(Creep fingers up one arm)
'It's time for a winter's nap,' says she.
(Pretend to yawn)
So under a leaf she began to creep,
(Place one hand over the opposite fist)
Spun a cocoon and fell asleep.
(Spin around once and lay head on hands)
Then spring came along one day and said,
(Shape arms in a circle like a sun)
'Wake up, wake up, little sleepyhead.'
(Finger on mouth in a whispering motion)

So she opened her eyes on a sunny day,
(Rub eyes)
Flapped butterfly wings and flew away.
(Hook thumbs, spread fingers and fly away)

Choose a child to remove the instructions from the 'We can' can. Recite the poem and do the actions as a group.

Chat about
Chat about a time when the children saw a caterpillar or a butterfly. Can they think of other things that change colour or shape? (NB: Ensure that they know not to touch caterpillars.)

Food fun

Butterfly sandwiches

> **Time guide: 10 minutes**
>
> **You will need:** Bread and butter, spreads such as butter, jam or cream cheese, toppings such as grated or sliced cheese, bananas cut into rings, raisins, pieces of celery or sliced meat, a plastic knife and a plate for each child

Give each child a slice of bread on a plate and a plastic knife. Help them cut their slices into two or four triangles and form butterfly shapes. Help them choose a spread for their bread and then a topping to decorate their butterflies. Eat up and clean up.

Chat about
Chat about what the children like best about butterflies. I wonder how long it takes for a caterpillar to change into a butterfly? If the children could change into something else, what would they change into?

Prayer pocket

'Thank you' trees

> **Time guide: 5 minutes**
>
> **You will need:** A prayer pocket decorated like a leaf, fallen leaves, 'thank you' paper (see photocopiable sheet on page 73), wax crayons, scissors, tape and a small twig for each child

Put the leaves in the prayer pocket before the session. When it is time, ask one of the children to remove them. Ask the children to think about someone who has helped them to grow. Perhaps it is someone who feeds them, helps them get dressed or plays with them. Perhaps it is someone who helps them learn about God, reads to them from the Bible or helps them to pray.

Explain that you are going to use the leaves to make a 'thank you' tree for the person that they are thinking of. Give each child a piece of 'thank you' paper (see photocopiable sheet on page 73), a leaf and some crayons. Place the leaf underneath the paper (words side up) and colour over it with a crayon until the leaf pattern shows through. Make as many different kinds and colours of leaves as desired. Give each child a pair of scissors and a twig. Help them to cut out each 'thank you' leaf and attach it to the twig with tape.

Chat about

Chat about who the children will give their 'thank you' tree to. Why do they want to thank God for this person? How does this person help them to grow?

Finish with the following prayer.

Thank you, God, for loving me so,
Thank you, God, for helping me grow! Amen

Home and away link

Send the 'thank you' trees home with each child. 'Home and away' provides a further linked activity.

Busy box

Paper plate sunflowers

 Time guide: 10 minutes

You will need: One paper plate per child, yellow paint, paintbrushes, sunflower seeds, lentils, PVA glue, green garden sticks

Help the children to paint their plates yellow and let them dry. Apply glue in the middle of the plates and sprinkle with sunflower seeds and lentils. Once dry, tape the flowers to the garden sticks.

Chat about

Chat about what we need to do to help seeds grow. What do we need ourselves to grow healthy and strong?

Go game

Birds' nests

 Time guide: 5 minutes

You will need: One plastic hoop and beanbag for each child, a bird call or whistle for the leader

Put the beanbags in a pile in the centre of the room and the hoops at equal distances around it. Assign each child a hoop and ask everyone to stand inside his or her hoop. Explain that they are birds, their hoops are nests and the beanbags are eggs. When the leader blows the whistle, the birds are to run to pick up an egg and return it to their nest. When the whistle is blown again, they are to try to steal eggs one at a time from other nests while protecting their own from being stolen. They must only steal one egg at a time and it must be placed carefully in the nest, not thrown from a distance. When a bird has collected three eggs, they must sit down on their eggs and shout 'Bird's nest!'

Chat about

Chat about a time when the children saw a bird's nest, a bird's egg or a baby bird.

Music makers

Caterpillar, butterfly

 Time guide: 5 minutes

You will need: Some garden-themed or classical music and a leader

While the music is playing, the children are to fly about the room like butterflies. When the music stops, they are to drop to the ground and wiggle like caterpillars.

Memory time

 Time guide: 5 minutes

You will need: The Bible verse 'Keep on growing with God' (2 Peter 3:18b, paraphrased)

Teach the children the following actions. Explain that remembering what is said in the Bible can really help us, and that they are going to try to remember something the Bible says, using both words and actions.

Keep on: Fingers in a 'C' shape in front of you, sweeping out in both directions.

Growing: Move right hand from waist height into the sky.

With God: Point up to God.

Practise the actions to the verse yourself in advance of the session.

Chat about

Chat about what it means to grow with God.

Home and away

Give each child a copy of Home and Away Sheet 10 (see page 83) and a copy of the 'We have a little garden' rhyme time poem (see page 93) if desired.

Name tag templates

Crab

Dog

Cow

Teddy

Crow

Lamb

Donkey

Pig

Cat

Caterpillar

Good Sammy stick puppet templates

Crooked man

Robber

Busy Bob

Wallace

Good Sammy

Nurse

'Thinking of you' teddy template

Matching animals

Purse-shaped template

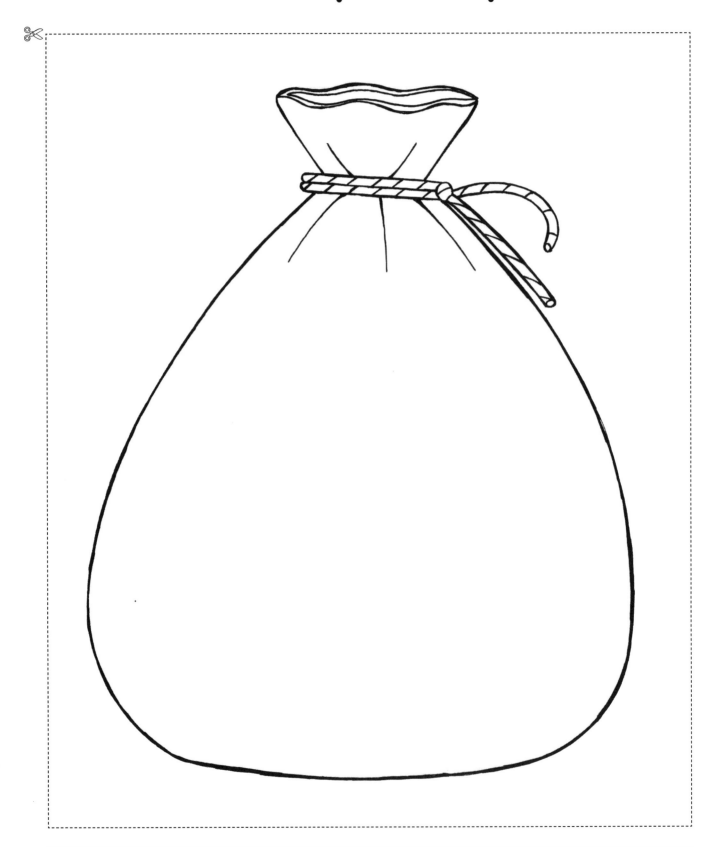

Seaside prayer shapes

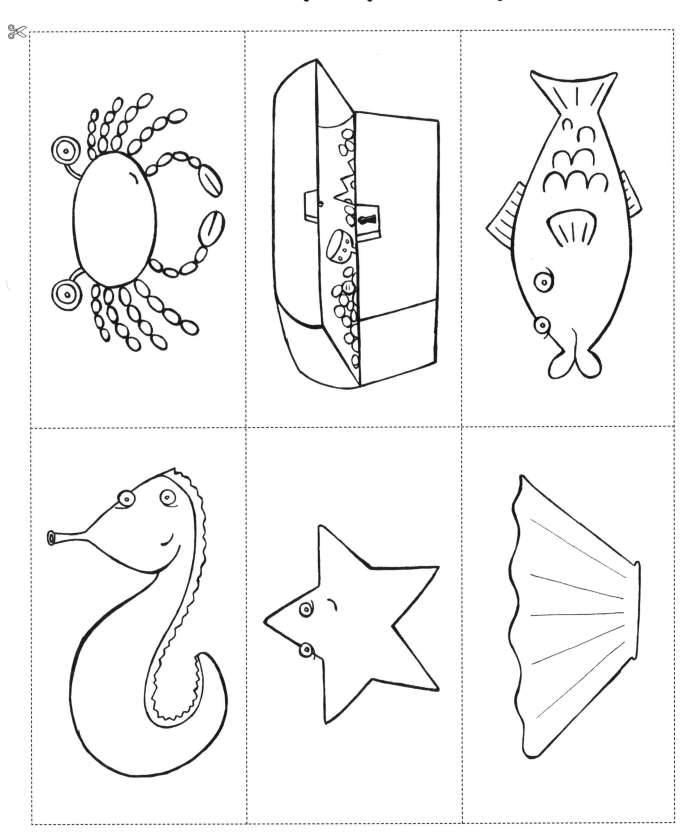

Wordless prayer book

Card houses and prayer bricks

Door Thank you for my friends	**Kitchen** Thank you for my food
Living room Thank you for my family	**Bedroom** Thank you for my bed

Reproduced with permission from *Parable Fun for Little Ones* published by BRF 2007 (978 1 84101 491 3) www.barnabasinschools.org.uk

Share-a-prayer cards

Please help my friend to feel better.

Please help my friend to be brave.

Please be close to my friend.

Please give my friend what they need.

Please help my friend not to worry.

Please help my friend to
know what to do.

Thank you paper

ank you.Thank you.Thank you
Thank you.Thank you.Thank y
ank you.Thank you.Thank you
Thank you.Thank you.Thank y
ank you.Thank you.Thank you
Thank you.Thank you.Thank y
ank you.Thank you.Thank you
Thank you.Thank you.Thank y
ank you.Thank you.Thank you
Thank you.Thank you.Thank y
ank you.Thank you.Thank you
Thank you.Thank you.Thank y
ank you.Thank you.Thank you
Thank you.Thank you.Thank y

Reproduced with permission from *Parable Fun for Little Ones* published by BRF 2007 (978 1 84101 491 3) www.barnabasinschools.org.uk

The parable about a hidden treasure

Thank you for sharing your child(ren) with us today. Here are some of the things we thought about together and some things you might like to try at home.

Think together

Today's story and activities were based around Jesus' parable about a hidden treasure.

Jesus said: The kingdom of heaven is like what happens when someone finds treasure hidden in a field and buries it again. A person like that is happy and goes and sells everything in order to buy that field.

MATTHEW 13:44

Link together: Seaside bangle

You will need: The sheet(s) of sea shapes your child(ren) brought home today, scissors, colouring crayons, hole punch, uncooked pasta tubes, shells, a length of ribbon or string

Help your child(ren) cut out and colour the shapes and punch a hole for threading. Thread the pasta tubes, beads, shells and paper shapes on the ribbon or string and tie to make a seaside bangle.

Play together: Hunt the treasure

You will need: A box full of treasure (a mixture of costume jewellery, coins, chocolate coins, small toys and so on), a really long piece of string

Without the child(ren) seeing, tie one end of the string around the treasure box and hide it out of sight (under a pile of cushions, clothes or toys or outside under a bush). Trail the string around the room or outside (over and under furniture or plants, out the door, up the stairs and so on). When the child(ren) arrive(s) give them the loose end of the string and help them to follow it to the treasure, delighting in the items on the way. Explore and enjoy the contents of the treasure box together.

Pray together
Thank you for treasuring me.
Help me to treasure you. Amen

Reproduced with permission from *Parable Fun for Little Ones* published by BRF 2007 (978 1 84101 491 3) www.barnabasinschools.org.uk

The parable about the growing seeds

Thank you for sharing your child(ren) with us today. Here are some of the things we thought about together and some things you might like to try at home.

Think together

Today's story and activities were based around Jesus' parable about the growing seeds.

Jesus said: God's kingdom is like what happens when a farmer scatters seed in a field. The farmer sleeps at night and is up and around during the day. Yet the seeds keep sprouting and growing, and he doesn't understand how. It is the ground that makes the seeds sprout and grow into plants that produce grain. Then when harvest season comes and the grain is ripe, the farmer cuts it with a sickle.

MARK 4:26–29

Link together: Farm fun wind chimes

You will need: The farm wind chime(s) your child(ren) brought home

Hang the wind chime in the garden.

Chat about

Chat about how the wind feels. How does the wind sound?

Play together: Tom Farmer grass head

You will need: One leg of an old pair of tights for each child, a plastic container or yoghurt pot, scissors, tablespoon, moist potting mix, stickers, felt pens, grass seed

Hold the stocking open. Insert at least three tablespoons of grass seed and three to four cups of moist potting mix. Knot the stocking securely above the potting mix and shape it into a round 'head'. Place it in the container. Let the child(ren) make a face on the grass head and use stickers for buttons or a tie. Keep the grass head damp and it will begin to grow hair in a few days.

Chat about

Chat about what farmers do.

 Pray together
Lord, help us to grow day by day, to be more like you in every way. Amen

Reproduced with permission from *Parable Fun for Little Ones* published by BRF 2007 (978 1 84101 491 3) www.barnabasinschools.org.uk

The parable about a farmer

Thank you for sharing your child(ren) with us today. Here are some of the things we thought about together and some things you might like to try at home.

Think together

Today's story and activities were based around Jesus' parable about the farmer.

A farmer went out to scatter seed in a field... Some of the seeds fell along the road and were stepped on or eaten by birds. Other seeds fell on rocky ground and started growing. But the plants did not have enough water and soon dried up. Some other seeds fell where thorn bushes grew up and choked the plants. The rest of the seeds fell on good ground where they grew and produced a hundred times as many seeds...

This is what the story means: The seed is God's message, and the seeds that fell along the road are the people who hear the message. But the devil comes and snatches the message out of their hearts, so that they will not believe and be saved. The seeds that fell on rocky ground are the people who gladly hear the message and accept it. But they don't have deep roots, and they believe only for a little while. As soon as life gets hard, they give up.

The seeds that fell among the thorn bushes are also people who hear the message. But they are so eager for riches and pleasures that they never produce anything. Those seeds that fell on good ground are the people who listen to the message and keep it in good and honest hearts. They last and produce a harvest.

LUKE 8:5–8, 11–15

Link together: Wordless prayer book

> **You will need:** The wordless prayer book(s) your child(ren) made today

Encourage your child(ren) to tell you about God's love using the wordless book.

Chat about

Chat about the different colours in the prayer book.

- ✪ Grey apple: We all do wrong things
- ✪ Red apple: Jesus loves us
- ✪ White apple: God forgives us
- ✪ Gold apple: God plants his seed of love in us
- ✪ Green apple page: We grow to be like Jesus

Play together: Make a scarecrow

> **You will need:** An old pillowcase, trousers, long-sleeved shirt, hat, broom handle, boots, gloves, packing material (newspaper, foam or straw), coloured pens, paper, PVA glue, string

Build a scarecrow. Make a face on one side of the pillowcase using pens, paper and glue. Tie the gloves to the shirt sleeves and the boots to the trouser legs using string. Stuff the scarecrow with the packing material, put a hat on its head, attach it to the broom handle and stick it in the garden.

 Pray together
Lord God, thank you that your love is found in our hearts and all around.

Reproduced with permission from *Parable Fun for Little Ones* published by BRF 2007 (978 1 84101 491 3) www.barnabasinschools.org.uk

The parable about the good Samaritan

Thank you for sharing your child(ren) with us today. Here are some of the things we thought about together and some things you might like to try at home.

Think together

Today's story and activities were based around Jesus' parable of the good Samaritan.

As a man was going down from Jerusalem to Jericho, robbers attacked him and grabbed everything he had. They beat him up and ran off, leaving him half dead.

A priest happened to be going down the same road. But when he saw the man, he walked by on the other side. Later a temple helper came to the same place. But when he saw the man who had been beaten up, he also went by on the other side.

A man from Samaria then came travelling along that road. When he saw the man, he felt sorry for him and went over to him. He treated his wounds with olive oil and wine and bandaged them. Then he put him on his own donkey and took him to an inn, where he took care of him. The next morning he gave the innkeeper two silver coins and said, 'Please take care of the man. If you spend more than this on him, I will pay you when I return.'

Then Jesus asked, 'Which one of these three people was a real neighbour to the man who was beaten up by robbers?'

The teacher answered, 'The one who showed pity.'

Jesus said, 'Go and do the same!'

LUKE 10:30–37

Link together: Good Sammy stick puppets

You will need: Stick puppet templates that your child(ren) brought home today, coloured crayons, scissors, craft sticks, tape

Help your child(ren) to colour and cut out their stick puppet templates. Attach each one to a craft stick with the tape. Use the stick puppets to retell the story.

Play together: First aid fun

You will need: A willing volunteer (or toys and teddies), bandages, plasters, lotion, notepad and pencil, ice cubes, toy doctor's kit

Play hospital and let your child be a 'Good Sammy'. Make ice cubes (use food colouring for added enjoyment) and use them to treat play bumps on the head.

 ## Pray together
Thank you, Lord God, for the people who take care of others. Help them to be brave and strong. Help us to help others, too. Amen

Reproduced with permission from *Parable Fun for Little Ones* published by BRF 2007 (978 1 84101 491 3) www.barnabasinschools.org.uk

The parable about a lost coin

Thank you for sharing your child(ren) with us today. Here are some of the things we thought about together and some things you might like to try at home.

Think together

Today's story and activities were based around Jesus' parable about a lost coin.

What will a woman do if she has ten silver coins and loses one of them? Won't she light a lamp, sweep the floor, and look carefully until she finds it? Then she will call in her friends and neighbours and say, 'Let's celebrate! I've found the coin I lost.' Jesus said, 'In the same way God's angels are happy when even one person turns to him.'
LUKE 15:8–10

Link together: Grandma's memory book

You will need: The memory book(s) your child(ren) brought home today

Fill the pages with photos, drawings, flower pressings and so on, and give it to Grandma or a grandma figure.

Chat about

Chat about who is in your family. What do(es) your child(ren) like best about their family?

Play together: What's missing?

You will need: Several household items and a coin

Place all the items on a table and cover them with a towel. Take the towel away and give the child(ren) a minute to try to memorize what items are on the table. Cover everything up with the towel again and ask the child(ren) to remember as many things as they can. After a while, start taking an item away and guessing what has been removed. The game is over when you have removed the coin.

Pray together
Lord God, you remember me, you remember me. Help me to remember you as you remember me. Amen

Reproduced with permission from *Parable Fun for Little Ones* published by BRF 2007 (978 1 84101 491 3) www.barnabasinschools.org.uk

The parable about the two builders

Thank you for sharing your child(ren) with us today. Here are some of the things we thought about together and some things you might like to try at home.

Think together

Today's story and activities were based around Jesus' parable of the two builders.

Jesus said: Anyone who comes and listens to me and obeys me is like someone who dug down deep and built a house on solid rock. When the flood came and the river rushed against the house, it was built so well that it didn't even shake. But anyone who hears what I say and doesn't obey me is like someone whose house wasn't built on solid rock. As soon as the river rushed against that house, it was smashed to pieces!
LUKE 6:47–49

Link together: Card houses and prayer bricks

You will need: The card house(s) and prayer bricks your child(ren) brought home today

Use the prayer bricks to take a prayer walk around your home.

Play together: Dens

You will need: Items to make a den, such as blankets, sheets, rugs, broom handles, chairs, clothes horses and a table; an empty shoebox

Make a den together. Read a book, play a game, listen to music or have a picnic inside. Dismantle the den and put it up again, making improvements. Cut a slit in the top of the shoebox and pretend it is a letterbox. Write messages and send them to your child(ren).

Pray together
Help us to trust you, Lord Jesus.
Make us strong in all we do,
Help us to build our lives for you. Amen

The parable about prayer

Thank you for sharing your child(ren) with us today. Here are some of the things we thought about together and some things you might like to try at home.

Think together

Today's story and activities were based around Jesus' parable about prayer.

Then Jesus went on to say: Suppose one of you goes to a friend in the middle of the night and says, 'Let me borrow three loaves of bread. A friend of mine has dropped in, and I don't have a thing for him to eat.' And suppose your friend answers, 'Don't bother me! The door is bolted, and my children and I are in bed. I cannot get up to give you something.'

He may not get up and give you the bread, just because you are his friend. But he will get up and give you as much as you need, simply because you are not ashamed to keep on asking.

So I tell you to ask and you will receive, search and you will find, knock and the door will be opened for you. Everyone who asks will receive, everyone who searches will find, and the door will be opened for everyone who knocks.'
LUKE 11:5–10

Link together: Share-a-prayer cards

> **You will need:** The share-a-prayer cards that your child(ren) brought home and the 'thinking of you' teddy card(s)

Use the share-a-prayer cards to talk to your child about who needs prayer, and encourage them to give the 'thinking of you' teddy away to appropriate people.

Chat about

Chat about the things that your child(ren) would like to pray about.

Play together: Bedtime go-togethers

> **You will need:** Things that go together at bedtime, such as sock and shoe, pillow and pillowcase, left and right slippers, brush and comb, toothbrush and toothpaste and so on

Mix all the items together and help the children match them up as quickly as possible.

Pray together
Dear God, thank you that I can talk to you whenever I want. Amen

Reproduced with permission from *Parable Fun for Little Ones* published by BRF 2007 (978 1 84101 491 3) www.barnabasinschools.org.uk

The parable about the lost sheep

Thank you for sharing your child(ren) with us today. Here are some of the things we thought about together and some things you might like to try at home.

Think together

Today's story and activities were based around Jesus' parable about the lost sheep.

Then Jesus told them this story: If any of you has a hundred sheep, and one of them gets lost, what will you do? Won't you leave the ninety-nine in the field and go and look for the lost sheep until you find it? And when you find it, you will be so glad that you will put it on your shoulder and carry it home. Then you will call in your friends and neighbours and say, 'Let's celebrate! I've found my lost sheep.'

Jesus said, 'In the same way there is more happiness in heaven because of one sinner who turns to God than over ninety-nine good people who don't need to.'

LUKE 15:3–7

Link together: Matching animals

> **You will need:** The matching mother and baby animal pictures that your child(ren) brought home, and some music

Place the baby pictures face-up in a circle on the floor and divide the mother pictures between the players (one or more). The players circle around the outside of the baby pictures while the music is playing. When the music stops, the players must find the matching baby and put the mother beside it.

Chat about

Chat about what you like best about being together.

Play together: Sheep safari

> **You will need:** A child's room, a torch, party hats and poppers, a bedtime snack and lots of soft toys including a sheep

Hide the animals all over the room without the children's knowledge. Turn out all the lights. Pretend you are shepherds looking for your lost sheep. Lead the children in a sheep safari using the torch. Make the noise or action of each animal as you find it. Pile them high on top of the bed and have a party with the hats, poppers and snack when you find your lost sheep. (NB: Find the sheep last of all.)

 Pray together
Lord Jesus, thank you for being my good shepherd. Thank you for loving me. Amen

Reproduced with permission from *Parable Fun for Little Ones* published by BRF 2007 (978 1 84101 491 3) www.barnabasinschools.org.uk

The parable about the lost son

Thank you for sharing your child(ren) with us today. Here are some of the things we thought about together and some things you might like to try at home.

Think together

Today's story and activities were based around Jesus' parable about the lost son.

Once a man had two sons. The younger son said to his father, 'Give me my share of the property.' So the father divided his property between his two sons.

… The younger son packed up everything he owned and left for a foreign country, where he wasted all his money in wild living. He had spent everything, when a bad famine spread through that whole land. Soon he had nothing to eat.

He went to work for a man in that country, and the man sent him out to take care of his pigs. He would have been glad to eat what the pigs were eating, but no one gave him a thing.

Finally, he came to his senses and said, 'My father's workers have plenty to eat, and here I am, starving to death! …'

The younger son got up and started back to his father. But when he was still a long way off, his father saw him and felt sorry for him. He ran to his son and hugged and kissed him.

The son said, 'Father, I have sinned against God in heaven and against you. I am no longer good enough to be called your son.'

But his father said to the servants, 'Hurry and bring the best clothes and put them on him… This son of mine was dead, but has now come back to life. He was lost and has now been found.' And they began to celebrate.

LUKE 15:11–24 (ABRIDGED)

Link together: I spy binoculars

You will need: The binoculars your child(ren) brought home today

Go on a walk together and describe what you see in your binoculars.

Chat about

Chat about who you would like to invite for a visit. Who would you like to go and see?

Play together: Tape city

You will need: Masking tape, scissors, old catalogues, toy people, cars, farm animals

Help your child(ren) to create a city map on the floor using masking tape. Include roadways, parks, an airport, library, hospital, shops, garage and an outlying farm. Cut pictures from the catalogues to decorate: barn for the farm and so on. Accessorize with toy people, plastic animals and dolls' house furniture. Retell the parable using the tape city.

Chat about

Chat about how to cross roads safely. What do we do when we are approached by strangers? What would we like to see in the town or the country?

Pray together
I thank you, God, for what I see.
Thank you, God, for watching me!

Reproduced with permission from *Parable Fun for Little Ones* published by BRF 2007 (978 1 84101 491 3) www.barnabasinschools.org.uk

The parable about a mustard seed

Thank you for sharing your child(ren) with us today. Here are some of the things we thought about together and some things you might like to try at home.

Think together

Today's story and activities were based around Jesus' parable about a mustard seed.

Jesus said, 'What is God's kingdom like? What can I compare it with? It is like what happens when someone plants a mustard seed in a garden. The seed grows as big as a tree, and birds nest in its branches.'
LUKE 13:18–19

Link together: 'Thank you' trees

> **You will need:** The 'thank you' tree(s) that your child(ren) brought home today

Take your child(ren) to visit the person for whom the tree was made and give it to them as a present. If it is not possible to visit, take a picture of the tree and send this instead, remove the leaves and send them in the post, or put the tree somewhere special in your house.

Play together: Bird seed cake

> **You will need:** Wild bird seed, sunflower seeds, oats, peanuts, dried bread, lard, clean yoghurt pots, twigs, rope (heavy string or ribbon) and a teddy or other soft toy (one that doesn't mind being out in the rain)

Help your child(ren) to mix the seeds, oats, nuts and bread together in a bowl. Melt the lard on a low heat and add the dry mixture. Help your child(ren) to spoon the bird seed cake into yoghurt pots, pushing a twig into the middle for a handle. When the bird seed cake is completely set, remove it from the pot and tie it to a tree branch for the birds to eat. Tie one end of the rope around the teddy's waist and the other to a tree branch so that teddy swings about two feet off the ground.

 Pray together
Thank you, God, for loving me so.
Thank you, God, for helping me grow!
Amen

Reproduced with permission from *Parable Fun for Little Ones* published by BRF 2007 (978 1 84101 491 3) **www.barnabasinschools.org.uk**

Jolly Molly May

Maggie and Milly and jolly Molly May
Went to the beach to play one day.

Maggie found a shell that sang like the sea,
Went to show her mum, as happy as could be.

Milly found a crab scuttling all around,
Went to tell her dad what she had found.

I wonder, do you wonder, jolly Molly May,
What did you find on the beach that day?

Molly found a chest hidden in the sand,
Discovered it, uncovered it, then buried it again.

Molly's got a secret smile upon her face,
Molly's got a treasure and knows its hiding place.

I wonder, do you wonder, what our treasure is?
Jesus is our treasure and we are his!

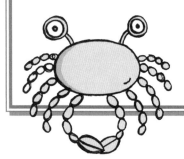

Reproduced with permission from *Parable Fun for Little Ones* published by BRF 2007 (978 1 84101 491 3) www.barnabasinschools.org.uk

Oats, peas, beans and barley grow

Oats, peas, beans and barley grow,
Oats, peas, beans and barley grow.
I wonder, do you wonder how
Oats, peas, beans and barley grow?

First Tom Farmer plants the seed,
Then he rests and takes his ease.
And while he's sleeping peacefully
Oats, peas, beans and barley grow.

Cockerel crows to sing the dawn.
Wake up, Tom, it's early morn!
Cows need milking in the barn
While oats, peas, beans and barley grow.

The horse needs hay, the pigs need corn,
The goat needs grass, the lambs are born,
The fence needs fixing, the hay is mown
While oats, peas, beans and barley grow.

Harvest time is nearly here,
Farmer Tom is full of cheer.
Hey, Tom, is it time to bring
The oats, peas, beans and barley in?

You and I can root and grow,
You and I can root and grow.
I wonder, do you wonder how
You and I can root and grow?

You and I grow day by day
Listening to what Jesus has to say.
God's Spirit helps us root and grow
When Jesus shows us the way to go.

Reproduced with permission from *Parable Fun for Little Ones* published by BRF 2007 (978 1 84101 491 3) www.barnabasinschools.org.uk

Farmer Friendly's simple deed

'Twas Farmer Friendly's simple deed
To scatter seed abundantly.

Some fell where it could not grow,
Got eaten by a big black crow.

Some sprang high in a rocky place,
Was withered by the sun's bright face.

Some fell among a crowd of weeds
That crushed and choked the growing seeds.

I wonder, do you wonder,
How will Farmer Friendly sow
To help the seeds take root and grow?

She ploughs her field, pulls out the weeds,
picks the rocks and plants the seeds.

In good soil the roots take hold.
The crops increase by hundredfold.

I wonder, do you wonder,
How will we sow
To help God's love take root and grow?

We'll pray a bit, we'll talk a bit,
We'll make a friend today.

Bit by bit God's crop will grow.
Away, you crows, away!

Good Sammy

There was a crooked man
Who walked a crooked mile,
Then a robber robbed him
And took away his smile!

Busy Bob bobbed along
But busied right on by.
Wallace wouldn't help,
Wouldn't even try.

I wonder, do you wonder,
Will anybody care?
Look! Here comes Good Sammy.
He's helping with a prayer.

He takes the man to hospital
Where he'll get much better,
Giving him some flowers
And a get-well letter.

I wonder, do you wonder
Who was a friend today?
Three cheers for Good Sammy.
Hooray! Hooray! Hooray!

Grandma Guddle's muddle

Old Grandma Guddle
is in such a muddle
And doesn't know what to do!
'Oh dear,' says she, 'I greatly fear
I have lost my penny.'

What? Lost your penny?
You poor old Granny.
Then she began to cry.
'Boo hoo, boo hoo, boo hoo, boo hoo.'
Then she began to cry.

'I once had ten but when I looked again
I couldn't find the one.'
I wonder, do you wonder,
Where has Granny's penny gone?

'I'll look,' says Granny, 'in every cranny!'
Then she began to spy.
'I spy, I spy, with my little eye.'
Then she began to spy.

She lifts the cat, looks under the mat,
Sweeps the floor with a broom,
Washes, dusts and polishes
In each corner of every room.

'It's uncanny,' says Granny.
'Where is my penny?
Oh where, oh where have I put it?
'Oh dear,' says she, 'see here, see here!
I've found it in my pocket!'

What? Found your penny?
Hooray for Granny!
We all begin to cheer!
Hooray, hooray, hooray, hurrah!
We all begin to cheer!

Old Grandma Guddle
gives Kitty a cuddle
Then phones a friend to say,
'I lost my penny, but now I have found it!
Oh what a busy day!'

I wonder, do you wonder,
Does God find us near or far?
Even when we think we're lost
He remembers where we are.

Mick and Mac

Mick is a builder,
Mac is too.
Building houses is what they do.

Mick is wise,
His plan is sound:
To build a house on solid ground.

Mick is thoughtful,
Knows the trick,
Lays a foundation brick by brick.

Mac is hapless,
Has no plan,
Decides to build on sandy land.

Mac is foolish,
Mac is thick,
Builds his shack quick, quick, quick.

Mick is happy,
Mac is too
Until a storm begins to brew.

I wonder, do you wonder,
Whether the weather will win?
Will Mac's shack come crashing in?

Walls do wobble,
Doors do creak.
'Eek,' says Mac, 'I've sprung a leak!'

Mumble, rumble,
Flash, boom, bash.
Mac's shack crumbles,
crash, crash, crash!

'Sorry Mac, mate,'
Says Mick to his friend.
'Come and stay with me
till the storm's at an end.'

I wonder, do you wonder,
How we too will win
When our worries come crashing in?

We'll ask Jesus
What's in God's plan.
When the storm hits us
he'll help us stand.

Now who is this a-tapping?

Now who is this a-tapping
On Tired Tim's door?
Tap tappit! Tap tappit!
At midnight or more?

Tired Tim's peeking out.
Pesky Pete's peeking in.
'Have you got any bread?'
He says with a grin.

'Pete, you're a pest,
please come back when it's day!'
I wonder, do you wonder,
Will Pete go away?

Now who is this a-tapping
On Tired Tim's door?
Tap tappit! Tap tappit!
Interrupting a snore!

Tired Tim's peeking out.
Pesky Pete's peeking in.
'The bread is for a friend,'
He says. 'Please let me in.'

'Please, Pesky Pete,
Come back when it's day!'
I wonder, do you wonder,
Will Pete go away?

Now who is this a-tapping
On Tired Tim's door?
Tap tappit! Tap tappit!
We've heard it before!

Tired Tim's peeking out.
Pesky Pete's peeking in.
'All right,' says Tim,
'There's some bread in my bin!'

I wonder, do you wonder,
Does God have a clock?
When we pray, night or day,
He is there when we knock.

Reproduced with permission from *Parable Fun for Little Ones* published by BRF 2007 (978 1 84101 491 3) www.barnabasinschools.org.uk

Good Shepherd had a little lamb

Good Shepherd had a little lamb
Whose fleece was white as snow,
And everywhere Good Shepherd went
The lamb was sure to go.

Then one day Good Shepherd woke.
His lamb he could not see.
I wonder, do you wonder,
Where Little Lamb could be?

Lamb, are you behind the tree?
Are you beside the stone?
Oh, Little Lamb, where are you?
You're lost and all alone!

Soon it will be night-time.
Shhh, there in the grass!
Good Shepherd's found his little lamb.
Happiness at last!

'I've found my lamb!' Good Shepherd says,
Laughing with a leap!
'Let's have a party right away
And invite the other sheep!'

I wonder, do you wonder,
Who might Good Shepherd be?
Jesus is the shepherd
Who cares for you and me.

Reproduced with permission from *Parable Fun for Little Ones* published by BRF 2007 (978 1 84101 491 3) www.barnabasinschools.org.uk

Silly Billy

Oh where have you been,
Billy boy, Billy boy?
Oh where have you been,
Silly Billy?

I have run away from home,
To the city I have gone,
And I have left my father.

What did you do,
Billy boy, Billy boy?
What did you do,
Silly Billy?

I threw a party, had some fun,
Forgot my father back at home.
But now my money is all gone.

Where do you live,
Billy boy, Billy boy?
Where do you live,
Silly Billy?

I'm very hungry and alone.
I eat with pigs, oh how I moan.
I miss my father and my home.

I wonder, do you wonder,
Billy boy, Billy boy?
Will he want you back again,
Silly Billy?

I know my father loves me so.
To God in heaven I will go
And say, 'Forgive me, father.'

Is he waiting by the gate,
Billy boy, Billy boy?
Is he waiting by the gate,
Silly Billy?

He is running, arms out wide,
Hugs and kisses, joy inside.
'Safe at last!' my father cried.

Does he want you to come in,
Billy boy, Billy boy?
Does he want you to come in,
Silly Billy?

There's a party just for me,
New clothes, a ring and tea.
I am back home with my father!

I wonder, do you wonder,
Billy Boy, Billy Boy?
Does God forgive every
Silly Billy?

Yes, God forgives us every one,
No matter what we've said or done.
God is a kind and loving Father.

We have a little garden

We have a little garden,
A garden all our own,
And every day we water there
The seed that we have sown.

And every day, no matter what,
We watch and wait and pray.
I wonder, do you wonder,
Will our seed grow today?

See, our seed is growing,
Our seed that was so small
Has grown into a nesting tree,
Big and strong and tall.

We are in God's garden,
He tends us with such care,
He warms us with his love
And waters us with prayer.

I wonder, do you wonder
What you and I will be?
Every day, no matter what,
We'll wait and pray and see!

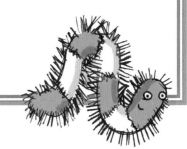

Index